THE BEAUTIFUL DARKNESS

A Handbook for Orphans

Joshunda Sanders

ISBN: 1537402021
ISBN 13: 9781537402024
Library of Congress Control Number: 2016914654
CreateSpace Independent Publishing Platform
North Charleston, South Carolina

For Edna, Jose, and Marguerite

TABLE OF CONTENTS

ACKNOWLEDGMENTS

I would not be a writer if it were not for my uniquely challenging and rewarding childhood. For that, I have to thank Marguerite Mary Sandoval, who gave me every bit of her sane moments to make sure that I knew what was possible even when it seemed like life was full of impossibilities and misfortune. My mother gave me the gift of faith, which has been essential to my life's work as a writer and to my development as a human being, a woman, and a black woman. From her, I also inherited a deep belief in the severe empathy that tragedy and heartbreak can bestow. I learned to laugh from my gut. I learned not to take anyone or anything for granted or to feel entitled to anything at all. Because of her, I am a fighter. I humbly stand tall and remember how hard she cheered for me, how she shouted from the rooftops about my greatness—and I remember that to do less than that because I am shy and I worry about sounding conceited is dishonor to her and to our God, so I grind. And I write. And I keep smiling, laughing, and remembering her along the way.

Kristen Mack, my sister, has been an advocate for this book for many years. So has Frank Bergon, one of my favorite and most enduring writing professors. Rita and Alphonso Scarborough and my friends—Vicki McClure, Emma Cheuse, Julian Lytle, Chazeman Jackson, Shequila Purnell-Saunders, Jennifer Gandin Le, stacia

l. brown, Mary Ann Roser, Portia Groce, Nicole Smith, and Ana Cantu and on and on and on—you all are the constellation, the array of light in my head as I write that reminds me that great things are expected and that you will read this work as it is rendered when it is ready because you believe that it should be in the world. Thank you for reminding me to be braver than I always feel—which is not brave, really, at all.

This book is for the adult children among us who never got to really be kids. It is for anyone who has had to raise their parents or the adults who were supposed to be there for them and somehow still turned out OK. It is a reminder that even the darkness in our lives prepares us to accept the light, that there is beauty in even the darkest things, if only we will allow ourselves not only to dream but to keep moving toward that dream without fail, with perseverance and strength.

INTRODUCTION

E xactly twenty years after my mother threatened to kill me, she was diagnosed with terminal cancer and given six months to live. I had to accept that even after I forgave her—if I could—I would always feel that I had been an orphan.

In my early thirties, for a span of three years, it felt like everything I had worked toward was beginning to unravel. This is the story of self-discovery, how the unraveling began, and how forgiveness helped me relearn resilience. It is a narrative reminder that some of our darkest moments can reveal the beauty of our lives to us, depending on what we decide to do with them.

In 2010, my estranged father, Victor, died by suicide.

In 2011, my mother, Marguerite, was diagnosed with Stage IV cervical cancer.

In 2012, Marguerite died six days before I turned thirty-four years old.

The combination of these events threatened to take me down, even after three decades of surviving so many other things. But there is nothing like losing the woman who brought you into the world. The shocking, sudden end to my mother's life nearly destroyed me. I had felt this kind of weariness before, the kind that sinks into both flesh and bone.

The difference was that before, my weariness was self-inflicted. When I didn't have to work three jobs and go to graduate school at night, I found myself confronted by a lot of free time and more energy than I knew what to do with, so I decided to train for a marathon. It was the same spring that I learned that Victor had died.

The timing of my first marathon in New York City could not have been better. I padded through those streets like the Clydesdale runner I have always been, remembering that I had walked so many of those streets with my mother, hungry and sometimes homeless. The race itself took me almost the length of a work day—nearly seven hours—my thighs bleeding and chafing, my heels sore, and the enormity of my accomplishment dwarfed by the reason I started running long distances to begin with: to forget my father's suicide several months before, to force myself to mourn like a normal person.

The next year, when Marguerite was diagnosed, I tried again to cope in a healthy way. I was both successful and unsuccessful. Even though I was in group therapy at the time, running by myself turned out to be the easiest and most cathartic experience—a way for me to decompress, to be alone with my feelings. Running gave me space to process my grief in necessary solitude.

But in running lingo, there is a point in a marathon called a wall. The wall is a mental block you encounter during a race of any length when you're not sure you'll be able to keep going. My life to that point had included a childhood stay in foster homes when I was five years old; multiple stays at family shelters, welfare hotels, and subsidized housing; and long stretches of abuse, hunger, confusion, and neglect.

I ran through these things first as a teenager, when I spent my first year in high school on a track team. I would go on to attend elite schools on scholarship, which saved me, affirmed my will to live, and gave life to my dream of writing for a living when I became a newspaper journalist. But after moving to seven cities in the course of five years, working a few jobs, and managing the rapid deterioration of my parents, by the time I hit my midthirties, I did not feel temporarily leveled or at all brave. I felt like I would never know myself again unless I changed. I was tired. I saw the wall, and instead of trying to run through or around it, I just stopped.

The self is all we ever have, especially the loners among us, the ones who are raised as, or are truly, only children. Because of this, to be felled by a harrowing emptiness and despair was as inevitable and dangerous as it was natural, my friends said. They brought me wine and breakfast tacos, they endured my incoherent sentences about the mundane that I tried to keep as a part of my internal dialogue. But I still felt confused by where I was, why I had been there, what I was supposed to do now.

For years, my answer to all hard things in life was to keep moving, physically and mentally. I believed I could run through it. For a while, that worked, as it always had. It had worked when I was a gangly freshman at Aquinas High School, where the basketball coach—bemused by my combination of height and impressive inability to play the sport—gently referred me to track and field, where I was christened Flo Jo for my speed. But if making the lottery for the New York City Marathon helped me suppress and ignore and literally run away from what I hoped was the last of my life's tragedies, then I figured that running more marathons would mean that nothing could break me permanently. Isak Dinesen's quote: "The cure for anything is salt water: sweat, tears or the sea," rang true. I was landlocked in Texas, and the sea was too far for the frequent visits I craved. But I could sweat anywhere and everywhere.

As for the tears, they held me over as I flew to San Francisco for the last full marathon I would be able to complete, a month after my mother was diagnosed with the cancer that would kill her six months later. It was a race that I finished by walking—texting a boy who was no good for me and yearning not just for the Tiffany finisher's necklace but an American Spirit cigarette.

Bad fortune, calamity, insanity—I can cope with these things. What I can't abide is feeling powerless. I don't really know how to be broken, even when I am, or what it means to stay there. It's another inevitability, I guess, but the vulnerability it requires feels like a death sentence. Each time I have been broken, it has felt like the end of the world. I have been given gifts that impart the trite wisdom of caterpillars and cocoons and becoming a butterfly, and I am both endeared to the people who repeat these things and inclined to hide my impulse to wretch in response.

I decided when I was little that I would not let anything break me beyond the ability to rise in repair. I restated this vow to myself again when I was a runner in earnest, even sporadically. This is how runners persevere, how we move through life. We decide we can do what most people believe is impossible, so we do it.

I am proud of that impulse for self-preservation. I think we all have it, but for some of us it is harder to deploy than for others. And even though I'm not comfortable with being broken, I have come closer to breaking than I knew possible. The years, the cities, the people: they have been heavy enough to make me bend. The weight of experience suggests that parts of me have been broken, even if I reject the idea of staying that way. This rejection didn't begin with my parents but ended with them. I like to think they would have approved.

No one can answer the question, though, of what their parents' approval is worth. After all, one right after the other, natural as the shift from fall to winter, my parents left me here. They'd left before: my father took his presence as well as his approval...along with any hope that we could forge something normal after meeting for the first time at my high school graduation. My mother took her suffocating love and infectious laugh by refusing medication that kept both from being replaced by demonic rage, the kind of anger that led to her choking me and threatening to end my life.

But this permanent, physical leaving is so different, even now, more than three years later. It's not just that the people who made me are no longer here but that the people most likely to believe the most beautiful and true things about me can no longer tell me so. The safe harbor of affection and joy that distinguishes parents—no matter how challenged or challenging they are—from anyone else was destroyed by their deaths, even if the only comfort I had was knowing that as long as they were alive, we might eventually get there together.

I miss, every day, what we could have become. The searing sensation of loss is a unique blend of faint heartburn and nausea throbbing in my flesh like a nagging injury that will forever resist recovery. My heart reaches for hope, cheer, and the normal vacillations of a full, complete life, but it always settles back in my chest empty, missing something.

You know when you are broken and damaged as a kid that maybe you will never live a life where you feel as adjusted and anchored in the world as the ones who were never harmed, who were always protected. But the dreamer in me, the optimist warrior, loves choosing hope. My heart is the underdog I'm always rooting for.

CHAPTER 1

STAY READY

All I have ever wanted to be was a writer, but more times in my life than I want to admit, I have silenced myself, unsure about whether some things weren't better unrecorded.

My desire to write emerged first when I was twelve. I needed a friend, a cheap and easy way to order my world. I don't remember a time during my childhood when my young life wasn't out of order, marked by my mother's mental illnesses, which I didn't learn about until I was an adult. Between 1984 and 1991, we were frequently homeless in Philadelphia and in New York. We were the poorest people I knew, and we frequented church food pantries at least twice a month. Beyond the poverty, my mother was sometimes viciously abusive, both physically and verbally.

Writing it all down with pens that were borrowed or stolen in notebooks from mom's failed night school explorations became my one constant. When I applied for scholarships to boarding school and college, prompted by questions about what I had learned from my experiences, I put my heart on the page, and it felt better than confession. I learned the power of my story this way, by the reaction of the many visible and invisible people who would shape my destiny by reading it.

I wrote everything—poems, five-year plans, ten-year plans. If I had a plan for my writing career, I don't remember what it was. I could not have predicted that I would publish my first poem when I was still a teenager, or that my quiet obsession with recording the details of author lectures open to the public on college campuses would lead to a stint as a writer and editor on my college newspaper. I did not fully understand the impact of putting my heart on the page for an audience besides myself when I wrote about volunteering at a prison as a Vassar student from the Bronx, a girl who had more in common with the black and Latino men who were part of a prerelease program I participated in than the children of the rich and famous who happened to be my classmates.

My journalism career had been launched by breaking what I was to learn was a cardinal sin in journalism—being unapologetically subjective. My life was such that I could not help but share my point of view, though I would learn to tone it down and hold it in. In a journalism career that spanned seven cities and five newspapers, I found a way to use my passion for writing in service to other people while also making a living and supporting myself.

Journalism allowed me to write myself out of poverty and into the working class. Along the way, I found my tribe—a group of friends and colleagues who astounded me with their humor, brilliance, and commitment. Newspaper journalism also fed the part of me that was attracted to an unpredictable life. For my first career, it made sense that I had found my way into a universe where my coworkers and my deadlines were the only constant—and even those things had the nerve to shift sometimes.

In Texas, I had a chance to deepen my reporting experience, which had only begun in earnest when I was finishing a newspaper fellowship in 2002. I had left California because I knew there remained so much for me to learn about reporting and writing that I couldn't learn at a large daily. So I moved to a smaller place.

In 2010, I had no idea that by the time 2011 was over, I would no longer be working as a newspaper reporter. My plan for landing a job at the *Austin American-Statesman* five years before had been to work the night cops job that I was overqualified for so that I could earn a library science degree, taking classes during the day. The newspaper and the people I worked with there felt like home.

The *Statesman* was, at the time, a substantial plot of land on the banks of Lady Bird Lake across Ann Richards Bridge from a tiny compact downtown—adjacent to the bridge home of the famous bats that took flight most of the year at sunset, drawing amazed crowds of tourists and terrifying local insect populations. The *Statesman* also had an excellent reputation in newspapers for the quality of journalism it produced as a midsized daily in the state capital. Yes, there were the quirks of Austin and the weirdos in it, but I was also drawn to what felt like an entrepreneurial spirit, a special kind of perseverance that defined the Lone Star State and our collective reporting as a result.

Texas was the last place I ever expected to find myself, but the state grew on me over time. All the things that I had loved about the Bronx—reliable and cheap public transportation; real liberals; a diversity of thought and ethnicity—were missing from the state. But right after college, at twenty-two, I learned how to navigate Houston's six-lane highways and to appreciate the culinary magic that is tortilla soup. In Beaumont, I learned the ways of Cajun folk and acquired a taste for Shiner and crawfish étouffée, even as I realized that I could not ever make a home in a part of East Texas where the Ku Klux Klan was active.

And in Austin, where I would find refuge for more than eight years, not only were the breakfast tacos good and the University of Texas replete with vast treasure troves of information and books, but I could also afford a house of my own. Buying a house was the biggest blessing that came from living in Texas. For a kid who had never even dared to dream of homeownership, it took a little time to get used to turning the key in my own lock, paying the mortgage, and putting plants in the ground—all without any drama. Great women like Barbara Jordan, Molly Ivins, and Ann Richards had also made their mark on the Lone Star State, and it felt good to be steeped in a culture where it was possible for badass women to thrive.

My dating life was relatively nonexistent except for episodic chaotic relationships with men from my past. I went to therapy. I ran. I made work and running my main marriage.

Then, on Earth Day in 2010, I received the phone call that would start the clock on the rest of the monumental life changes that I had no warning were on the horizon. I had picked up a Saturday afternoon shift, which was my least favorite of all the shifts I worked because it usually involved coverage of a least one festival. That April weekend was no different.

I had done a round of cop calls—routine checks to about sixty public safety officials in the Central Texas region—to make sure that we hadn't missed any major accidents since the last time we'd called them. I was gathering my things and picking up a reporter's notebook to head out of the empty newsroom when my desk phone rang. I was surprised to discover was that it was one of my father's seven sisters.

"I'm sorry to have to be the one to tell you this, but your father has passed away," she said.

I stood with the phone receiver tucked between my shoulder and my ear and let my notebook and my keys fall to my desk. The utilities company in Blackwood, New Jersey, had tried checking on the house weeks before my father's body had been discovered hanging in the garage. The tag they left on the door caught the attention of one of his neighbors, who then called the police. My sister Victoria told me later that inside his house were hundreds of photographs that he'd laid out on the coffee table, the living room fan sending flies from the garage to the sliding glass window.

"They say there are no signs of foul play, but we're not so sure," my father's sister said.

"Oh my God," I said, dropping back down into my seat with my head in my hands. I was crying; then I looked at the clock and wiped my eyes. I didn't ask her about funeral arrangements or anything else. I think she asked me for my address so they could send me a copy of the death certificate. "I have to go," I said, still in shock. "Thank you for calling and telling me."

I called my therapist, sobbing. She said something about shock and told me to take the time I needed to process. I went to my assignment, barely able to write anything sensible, but I tried. I went to a birthday lunch for an acquaintance, though I was visibly upset and needed to leave shortly after I got there because I was so troubled.

It was not the reaction I would have expected to have. I had a vague set of facts about my father, but I had only met him fourteen years prior. At the time he died, we were more like uneasy acquaintances than father and daughter.

That might have been what made his death all the more shocking.

⋙⋘

I first met my father by way of a letter. He wrote to me about halfway through my senior year of high school, at the end of 1995. I am both relieved and sad that I don't have copies of the letters I sent to him. The first one, prompted by my mother suggesting that my father wanted to know me and I should write to him when I was a junior, was more like a paper-heavy care package of sketches, poems, and copies of my grades. I had inherited my mother's penchant for overkill and oversharing. I wanted to convince him at the beginning that I was worth knowing even if I didn't really believe that about myself at the time, and his abandonment and distance suggested that he didn't either.

When months passed and I didn't hear from him, I followed up with a curt, one-pager that explained that while I wanted to know him, I didn't *need* to know him, since my life was going fine without him. If he wasn't going to respond, fuck him.

I still have the yellowed envelope and the handwritten letter he responded with. Despite everything that led up to and followed it, it remains one of my most prized possessions. It is the closest I came to understanding my father, the only version of an autobiography, to my knowledge, he would ever write:

Dear Joshunda:

I am writing this letter so that you may know more about me. First, I must tell you that I receive transcripts of your grades and comments of your instructors, which give me some insight into you. I read all with pride of your achievements and your character. I am truly sorry that I didn't take an active interest in you as I should have.

These words I write are meant as much for you as myself. As you grow older you will truly understand that there will be many setbacks and miscalculations as well as successes, all obstacles can be overcome, but time lost can never be recaptured.

I was born October 27, 1942 in Selma, Alabama. I have 7 sisters and one brother, we lived in a one-room house with no running water or electricity. There was an outside toilet with a pump for water. We had kerosene lamps and a wood stove for cooking and heat.

When I was seven, we moved to Ohio to live with my father, who had moved North to work in a rubber factory. I had not known my father for he had left when I was very young. I, like you, had been raised and nurtured by my mother.

My relationship with my father was non-existent. As a teenager, I had no yearning for a college education. I proceeded to attend a vocational high school, where I took drafting as a trade. Upon my graduation, I left Akron and moved to Los Angeles California to live with an older sister so that I could seek employment, for there was no work in Akron requiring any skills only manual labor.

After working as a print machine operator, I finally achieved my dream after quitting my first job and obtaining a job as a draftsman.

I worked at my trade for 4 years and was drafted into the U.S. Army. I spent two years in Panama working as a draftsman on communication systems. I enjoyed being in Panama and was thinking about staying but I knew that if I stayed, I would be a stranger in paradise.

So, upon my discharge, I returned to Los Angeles, I returned to work as a draftsman and I lived by myself, before I left I stayed with a sister and her husband, and then with my brother. I had promised my mother that I would not live by myself until I was twenty-one.

I worked two jobs and got a nice apartment and a sportscar. In 1967, I met my future wife. She became pregnant, and we married while she was four months pregnant.

I knew from the beginning that marriage was not for me, but I was willing to try. Our first child was Victoria. One year later, we had a son, Mark. I am a perfectionist who lives in the now, I loved my children, my feelings for my wife were mixed. I thought that a wife was to remain at home and raise the children. She believed otherwise. I wanted someone to do as I said (a learned behavior from my father, whom I hated).

My wife was from Long Island, New York who came from a upper middle class family and when I met her, she was attending college and living with her grandmother. Her parents didn't approve of our relationship or our marriage, which only added to our conflicts. After six years of marriage, I moved out and lived with my brother, I still continued to see my wife, I knew this was wrong and I must change the behavior for the sake of my children and to afford my wife a life of her own. I was thirty years old and going through an identity crisis. I bought a motorcycle and begin to ride with a group of guys. We would ride as a group on the weekends.

During this time, I met and fell deeply in love with a young lady who was visiting Los Angeles for the summer, she was from a rich family in Baltimore. Our summer ended and we communicated by phone and letter. I knew that I must leave Los Angeles to put some distance between my wife and myself for I would still see her. My chance came when I saw an ad in the newspaper for a job in Philadelphia.

I answered the ad and was flown to Philadelphia for a job interview. All was well, for I would only be a train ride away from Baltimore. I was accepted initially but I still was not sure, so I didn't accept. One month later, the company asked that I return for another interview. This time, I accepted. The first day on the job in 1974, I met your mother, who was a secretary assigned to walk me to another building in Center City.

I thought she was cute and nice, but not being aggressive, I kept my feelings to myself. I didn't like the people that I was working for and started looking for another job which I found, I left after six months. I kept contact with your mother. My friend in Baltimore and I drifted apart, she was attending the University of Maryland and we only saw each other once a year, which was not enough to sustain a relationship. In the meantime, my kids were attending school on Long Island and living with their grandparents.

They would visit me on the weekends, my son would spend part of his summer vacation with me. My wife and I kept contact by phone (We were now divorced, an action precipitated by her parents, she retains my last name.) I was busy at my career and going to discos and nightclubs. As time passed, I found that I was happiest being alone. I had the best of all worlds: I could go out and socialize and return home when I didn't want to be bothered (I was always selfish).

I have no true friends for I do not allow anyone close to me.

Upon the death of your mother's son, she and I saw each other frequently. I had moved from downtown Philadelphia to the West Side. During this time, I had lived with a lady who was a personnel director at an Insurance company, once again, I felt confined, even though I had my own room. Your mother and I saw each other once in a while. And when she informed me that she was pregnant with you, I was surprised for we had been seeing each other for four years. She told me that I was under no obligation.

I was not there at your birth, but I saw you as a baby, I remained distant from you and your mother until two years later when the apartment building I was living in caught fire. Your mother saw the news on television and came and told me that I could stay with her. I was deeply depressed for I had lost everything and I had no insurance. I stayed with your mother for two weeks, you maintained your distance from me as if you knew that I would fly away.

Even though I was grateful for your mother's helping hand, I needed at this time to be on my own. I regrouped and started again getting a new apartment. I didn't see you again for five years (Toby Farms). Your mother at that time was pursuing legal actions in her son's death. I was in and out of relationships. I was offered a job assignment for two years in Niagara Falls, New York in 1987.

I lost contact with your mother, upon my return in 1989, I quit my job in Philadelphia and moved to New Jersey where I had found another job. I heard from your mother and she told me about your going to school in Troy, New York. I received transcripts of your grades, but I was reluctant to contact you for if I were you, I would feel angry and abandoned. I am glad that you wrote me whether out of curiosity or commitment.

I don't know what our future holds, but I hope we keep in contact. There is much more to write but I will save it for some other time.

Love,
Your Father

Over the years, I must have read this letter more than twenty times. Each time, I am struck by the fact that he couldn't have been more honest and self-aware. He was very clear about who he was and the limitations of intimacy, friendship, and love in his life.

But I was, indeed, Marguerite's child. I was a relentless optimist and romantic, someone for whom feelings mattered more than reality. Combined with my stubbornness, I never believed there wasn't a closeness we could achieve if only I tried hard enough.

I met Victor on the morning of my high school graduation. A couple of my aunts, my sister, niece, and brother all came, along with my favorite cousin, Maria, and her husband, Lynell, who wore a plain white t-shirt beneath a casual-looking top. When he took off his over-shirt to reveal the Omega Psi Phi brand on his arm, I knew that Maria had found her soul mate, a man as gregarious as she.

The graduates were instructed to wear white dresses that bright, sunny day. Mine was a ten-dollar cream-colored faux lace number that nearly touched the tops of my feet. We were a vision, since the backdrop of our elegant dresses looked lovely with the vivid red roses we each held. Jane Fonda, an alum, spoke at our commencement ceremony.

Afterward, it became clear that I had acquired much more at Emma Willard than I had ever tried to carry by myself back to our Bronx apartment. Lynell and my brother, Manny helped load my things into piles in the parking lot. Somewhere in the midst of that commotion, I recognized the long face and long legs of my father in a taupe suit.

"Here you go," he said, handing me a box with a bow. I had asked for earrings as a graduation present, and he had obliged with a pair of gold hoops.

"Nice to meet you," I said.

"Yeah, right," he said.

After a post-graduation meal at a nearby Chinese restaurant, Dad drove Mom and me back into the Bronx. It was the only time

I had been in a car with both of them, and it felt like a scene out of a film. She was chattering from the backseat, complaining about how fast he was driving into the city.

"You could always walk," he said.

"Oh, Victor. You really know how to talk to a lady," she said, sucking her teeth and making sure her knees were closed beneath her floral dress.

"Yeah, right," he said, his voice close to a gruff whisper.

We rode the rest of the way in silence. When he dropped us back off in the Bronx, and once all my things had made it up the five flights, I wasn't sure whether to tell him I loved him or not.

"See you later," he said, as if he sensed my hesitation.

"OK," I said, relieved. "See you later."

The next time I saw him, it was for a summer trip to visit my grand-mother Betty in Ohio. He had told her and my other relatives about me shortly before the trip. She had a photo of me framed on a table with her other grandchildren. It was a gesture that felt like a gentle, wonderful equalizer. She gave me a hundred-dollar bill and said she was proud of me. It was our first and last meeting. She died during my freshman year at Vassar. Dad did not invite me to the funeral and, sensing he wouldn't say more, I didn't ask for any more details.

That was the summer my father and I drove up through New York to the Canadian border. We stopped in Buffalo for food and went to Canada, where he bought me a few new outfits before we stopped at the Canadian side of Niagara Falls. I leaned into the mist, marveling at the great gush of majestic, endless water.

"Don't stand too close," he said. "The water's polluted, you know."

I stepped back, confused. Was he just showing me his world so that he could keep the best parts of it to himself? Was this his version of bonding?

Instead of making introductions when we arrived in Akron, he let his sisters do all the awkward work. It wasn't awkward for long, since they noted my big, wide feet, which they all shared, and the same high cheekbones that obviously ran in the family. Dad disappeared, possibly to a hotel room where he was staying in the city. I hung out with my cousins Tracey and Phillip. Phillip was a saxophone player on his way to college, and I had such a crush on him immediately that I understood how and why people sometimes fell in love with and bred with their cousins.

I didn't see Dad again until it was time for him to drive Mom and me up to Vassar. I'd gone to visit once before—the arboretum was a beautiful, enchanted place full of exotic trees and exquisite old buildings. For the second and last time, I plopped down into the passenger seat with my mother and father in the car.

I relished every moment of it because the idea that both of my parents would be taking me to college shocked even me. It was a miracle that they had made me—I say that not because I feel particularly special or unique, but because they could not talk to or hear one another without bickering. I was soaking it all in, quietly as usual, as we packed up things I'd bought with my summer job money.

They argued like an old couple from the start of the trip. What was the best route? What music should we play? Whose fault was it that I was still sticking to this writing thing, anyway? It was a two-hour drive from the Bronx to Poughkeepsie, but it felt like four.

I stared out the car window for the whole trip, just as I had on our previous car trip together, only talking to him when he spoke to me. The trees were mostly green, but they were starting to turn gold and auburn and yellow. I couldn't wait to be alone in their midst, or at least in a quiet room where I could marvel uninterrupted at their beauty.

Mom was never OK with closed-in places, and it made me tired to feel her mind moving, constantly, behind me in Dad's maroon sedan. She fidgeted with her purse, just like she did on subways, rummaging for something, probably her house keys, at the bottom of her pleather purse. I wondered if feeling the press of metal in her hand grounded her with the feeling of having a place to return to. Sometimes I couldn't help but ask, "What are you looking for?"

She would answer me impatiently, aware that I was starting to get annoyed, and steady her hand, placing it on her lap with a fake smile that pulled at the corners of her full mouth tightly, her eyes wide. "Nothing, Shan. Nothing."

Victor had trimmed his beard, and even though I thought he was as strange as (if not more than) Mom, I could see what had attracted her to him. He was a closed book, with a padlock and a thick-linked chain wrapped around it. She must have found that mysterious and intriguing—a *Choose Your Own Adventure* for the deeply self-sabotaging romantic itch she could never quite scratch hard enough.

He was blasting Big Pun in the car. He turned up, "I Don't Wanna Be a Player," and Mom sucked the gap between her teeth. We were about twenty minutes into our adventure.

"Victor, why play this, man?" she snorted.

"It's my car," he said, without taking his eyes off the road. "You're leaving all this, huh?" he said to me without missing a beat.

I nodded.

"All kinds of good things in the Bronx you won't find at no Vassar."

"So what?" my mother said, continuing her defense. "So what. I know whose car this is."

"Act like it, then."

Mom's wig was on straight for a change, but her bangs frayed forward like a curtain billowing from a strong wind. Dad's Sunday best on the first day of college with his illegitimate daughter and her depressed mother was a pressed blue shirt and dark slacks. Mom was in her everyday outfit: a tight red shirt that struggled to press her breasts down and let her full belly fall under the tight black skirt.

They talked to each other that way for the next hour or so. At some point, Mom just leaned against the window and fell asleep. By the time we got to Poughkeepsie and I met my roommates at Strong, the all-girl's dorm on campus, I nearly flung myself in their arms before going to my corner of our small double room. I had a view of a quiet main strip on campus and a cluster of trees. I was safe and happy.

I was usually happiest when both Mom and Dad took off without me.

⇥⊹⊹⇤

Before I met Victor, I viewed Father's Day as an invitation to drink all day or stay in bed. Mom would call to cheer me up.

"I'm your mom and your dad," she would say. "Go on, wish me a happy Father's Day."

Even though I was more like *her* mom and dad, I said it anyway.

The more I learned about my father, the less I understood how he and Marguerite had ever been together. Victoria said they told her that he would often retreat to the basement of their home in Alabama for privacy. They called his house in South Jersey the Basement for that reason. No one went to visit because he never invited anyone to come over. He was the only person he ever intended to entertain there.

He had tried to keep me there, knowing that my mother's housing instability was a major challenge for me to deal with while trying to complete college. But he was, in fact, a recluse. He was most content on his own, without any interaction with anyone else.

While I was off chasing internships in New York City and Marguerite had gotten evicted from our last Bronx apartment, Victor let me move in. My things could be there, but when I was, he might refuse to say a word to me for days at a time. I did not tell him I expected him to pay the college bills that were sent to his home as soon as I changed my billing address. I would force him to take care of me in my passive-aggressive way.

He would park in the garage, walk into the house, and notice me on the couch writing on a laptop he had bought in the same spot where he used to watch television in the house that had previously been so relaxing; then he would say, "Have you moved all day?"

"I've been writing, Dad."

"You need a real job, one that pays money," he said, moving into the kitchen. The first week I stayed, he made salmon croquettes and white rice. The longer I was there, the less he did, though I never learned to cook. I was also stranded in the suburbs of New Jersey because I couldn't drive.

Rita, my older sister on my mother's side and the only relative that I was close to, was still abroad as a missionary. Everyone else was in New York.

"Writing is what I was born to do," I said to him, looking back at my computer to start again.

"No one is born to do anything," he said.

That was his final word on the subject.

This is why when he started to lose his eyesight, years after we had tried and failed during summers to live together, to build bridges of sentences and descriptions and trips over the many years and wounds that we hadn't shared, he probably decided that the only way to be free of having to live with other people or potentially depend on them was to die at his own hand.

He had worked so hard for his small, one-car garage house in a nondescript subdivision and the maroon car with the gray interior and manual controls on the steering wheel. He had worked so hard to get money so that he wouldn't have to deal with the world unless he wanted to and unless it was on his terms—rare for a black man—that as he aged into retirement and refused to answer my calls or letters, it must have only made sense for him to start his own end-of-life planning.

As for money, when it came time for me to move to Texas the first time after college, he handed me six hundred dollars. He bought me a flashy Raymond Weil watch. My thank yous may not have been profuse enough, but I was delighted. It was my first and only time feeling like a Daddy's girl. I packed up the small collection of books, some of my photos, some of my yearbooks.

"I'll come back for the rest," I said, dusting off my hands.

"You should take it all," he said, flatly. I ignored him while taking his money.

⪼⟊⪻

When I graduated from college, I took a newspaper fellowship with Hearst Newspapers that required me to move every six months for two years. After my father gave me that money, he told me the ATM was closed. I didn't talk to him again until two years later, when he called the newsroom where I was working in San Francisco to say, "I bet you thought I couldn't find your black ass."

"Dad? I'm at work. I can't talk right now," I said, whispering. I was relieved to hear from him but annoyed by his tone. "Can I give you my cell phone number?"

"I don't call cell phones."

I gave him my number anyway. He didn't call.

Several years later, when I had a couple of years left of library school, was holding down multiple jobs, and found myself at the end of an ill-fated romantic relationship that ended horribly, my father started e-mailing me at work to check on me. He told me nothing about what he was feeling or what his life was like. I was exhausted and depressed, and I said as much. I told him that even though I had a place of my own, it was mostly empty with bare walls and it would be even more lonely looking when my lover left.

He responded by sending me two beautiful framed prints that I immediately hung in the living room. Not long after that, he sent two boxes of books that I had left behind at his house during a few short stretches of time in college when I'd tried to make him be more like a normal father to me. The books came with a short letter that said there should be a truce between our houses now that he had sent my books back to me. The last e-mail I received from him was at the end of 2009 with the subject line "Remorse," that only said "I miss you."

My half-sister Victoria said that even though there were early conspiracy theories in his family that he might have been killed because of gambling debts, it was more likely that a diagnosis of glaucoma for a sixty-seven-year-old man who couldn't bear the thought of having to rely on people—let alone live with them—for the rest of his life factored into his suicide.

I kept going to therapy in Austin, but I could never bring myself to go to Blackwood. Instead, I trained for the New York City Marathon in the unrelenting heat that comes with Texas summer. It was my way of trying to outrun my anxiety, my sleeplessness. I was trying to run the pain in my heart and my gut out of my body.

It was strange to me, as I worked through my grief, that I had always assumed that my mother would be the one to commit suicide, not my father. I had believed he was the stronger of them, the one who had it together, despite his complicated feelings about our relationship. I went on to miss the stubborn absence of him, this man I loved for all of his potential, even when he refused to try or budge. I spent the early years of my childhood and then my womanhood longing for him to love me, only for the love to come with conditions I could never quite meet or understand.

In the immediate shock I felt after his death, I also remembered his uneasy smile and smelled those salmon croquettes. Victoria called to say that by the time the investigators found Dad's body, he had already started decomposing. They would have to clean and sell the house.

Because my father and I were not close, his final silence penetrated more deeply. I was angry with him for taking his life, and I didn't want to expose myself to the realities of his gruesome death while meeting the other members of his family at the same time.

I could not find nice things to say about my father when he died. He had worked for decades as an engineer, and his coworkers and even some of our relatives had nothing but sweet things to say about his sense of humor. "I have fond memories as a kid of him coming to town and always taking us to the toy store to get whatever we wanted," one of my cousins said in on online obituary. "He was a big inspiration to me...and he always encouraged me to keep learning. He will be sorely missed by the family!"

The family. *His* family. Did that include me?

The further away someone was from his inner circle, the sweeter he was to them, it seemed. One coworker said of him: "Vic was a good friend, an adopted family member and coworker of mine since 1974. My children grew up knowing Vic...he was loved by many, although a very private person. We miss you Vic, and we'll meet up again in the big design office on the other side."

These people had their reasons to love him, sure, but could they know that his own children—mainly me—did not grow up knowing him? It felt like my father had two lives, one that he opened up to the world that extended society's vision of him as a jolly giant of a man who was playful and funny and generous. The side he didn't show was a dark, loner personality. He had a penchant for shutting out people and his past for weeks and maybe months at a time, until he was forced to open up by some extreme event—a long-lost daughter, for example—to pretend to reconcile the two.

The reality of his death would continue to assert itself, by way of texts from Victoria or small checks from his estate. I still face it whenever suicide comes up in conversation or Father's Day approaches.

The news of my father's death only created in my mother a speechlessness that was suspicious for a woman who left consecutive voicemails when the phone cut her off. "OK," she said when I told her the news. "Well, OK. He's in a better place now."

"How are you feeling?" I asked, thinking, *Tell me that the love of your life just died and you are depressed. Say something, Marguerite. Say that you loved him and you didn't want him to die, and you're going to drink a lot to try and forget it.*

"I'm fine, Shan," was all she said. "We'll be fine."

Fine was a word my mother only used when she was pissed or devastated, so I worried. I had a right to worry, though I didn't know where the feeling was coming from or what would happen next. In the ensuing months, I worked three jobs. I barely slept. I tried all the online dating sites, all for naught. I was a shell of a human being, but I was trying to get sensation to return to my flesh. I wanted to feel alive again. Something, anything was better than the purgatory of being left behind.

I wonder if Mom decided to die then and just didn't tell me. At the end of 2011, I would get my answer.

CHAPTER 2

DECIDE WHAT FREEDOM
LOOKS LIKE

M y mother learned she had cancer not long after she turned
seventy. Her response to the cervical cancer diagnosis ex-
plains more than I can about her. Instead of doing what she had
always done—announcing the news to her family the way she an-
nounced that she had fallen in love with a new guy or had some
great new plans for a wealthy future—Marguerite locked herself in
her filthy Section 8 house in Philadelphia, curled up in her musty
bed that she'd had Manny move into the first floor dining room,
and waited to die.

I immediately felt that I could understand, even though I also
felt betrayed. Four of her five children were all grown and gone.
Victor was dead. She had lost everything and everyone she had
clung to in the world, or those things and people had been taken.

Seventy years of that was a long time. If there was a theme in
our conversations, it was my mother's eagerness to get to heaven.
When I was exasperated with her, tired, frustrated, and afraid, I
could only see that she was crazy, loud, and irritating. It was the
abusive, raging side of her that made me pray for her to die young.

To me, her death would offer freedom—from our impoverished past and from my ignorance of knowing how to cope with her while she was alive.

Getting distance from her and the many different facets of her personality allowed me to see how being a motherless child had left her without a role model to nurture me. We had been doomed, then, and the more I thought about the fact that what she had been missing she could not have then given to me, the easier it was for my heart to begin to soften. It got to be that I didn't appreciate her eagerness to die, and my lack of appreciation surprised even me.

Mom had been careless with her life because it had been careless with her. I had a child's hope that I was one big reason my mother could embrace life and get well and maybe be closer to what other women and mothers were. To be enough to save my mother from herself also felt like it could free us from more uncertainty.

It took decades to realize this was an impossible task. There was something missing that I could not find and give back to her. All the things that had abandoned her had left her long ago. In their place, she found random things to make her feel safe—and safety is the ultimate freedom.

Mom especially liked to collect paper. The presence of slips and scraps, usually religious, soothed her when she seemed beyond reach. At least until she got really sick, they kept her loneliness at bay.

When she decided that freedom to her looked like ending it all, nothing was consolation—not the stacks of Catholic hymnals and calendars scented and smeared with the burgundy lipstick she used until her plump pinky was scraping the bottom of the tube or the old envelopes stuffed with past due notices from student loans she never intended to pay back. When she was younger, when she'd had energy, she had written notes to God on walls that didn't belong to her. In the same perfect penmanship that had been shaped by her days writing shorthand as a secretary, she wrote me daily love notes on loose-leaf paper.

Now, even her written words showed her growing weak, the *M* in her name written as a wobbly line where it had once been a confident beam. In her dream life, she was building an empire of homes and gardens when the world arrived with the voice of a doctor to tell her that she was dying.

In the real world, Marguerite didn't own a single thing. She had never owned something that hadn't once belonged to someone else, aside from the occasional pair of cheap shoes or an extravagantly curly wig or new underwear. All her furniture and clothes were hand-me-downs, cast-offs. We never talked about it, but I wondered as I got older if she didn't feel that if she didn't have anything, nobody could take anything else away from her.

Her only triumph had been that once she'd had a house full of kids and, for a little while, a husband. She had tried to be a faithful woman of God, even when He took her son, Jose, perhaps especially then. There was *Before Jose* and *After Jose,* when living became its own kind of hell. Some people thought death was the end, but she knew better. Death had ruined her life, and now it was giving life back.

Death was starting to look like freedom.

For two weeks, Marguerite lay tucked inside old pissy sheets and blankets. She must have been so incredibly tired. Thirsty and hungry and lonely were nothing compared to how tired she was. If only she could just die in her sleep like this, slipping beyond like a pile of salt in the shadow of Sodom and Gomorrah.

It was dark in that little house, but the light in the world didn't offer her anything, either. She would be flirting with a handsome man asking him if she didn't favor Tina Turner (especially the legs!) and how much money she would get when she sued the taxicab driver that almost ran her over or the air force base that fired her or the last lawyer that took her money without filing a lawsuit, and someone might snicker nearby or tell her she looked like a man and she would pause, eyes blank, and remember that no one else lived in the world that existed in her head.

Her days began with her wide-eyed prayers to remain invincible and ended with despair that had sucked her tear ducts dry and made her want to open her veins with the razors she used to shave the callouses from her pinky toes and keep her eyebrows from growing back.

Prayer and the thought of her children kept her alive. Maybe God would perform one last miracle and just take her if she could just keep still, just surrender, in that bed. No hospitals. Her mother, Edna had died in a Poughkeepsie asylum when Marguerite was just a little girl, after she was poked and prodded and her insides were photographed.

No, Marguerite wanted to die like she had lived: On her own terms.

⊱——⊰

Marguerite was raised by her aunt, Johnnie Ann, a slight, four-foot-eleven woman who once flung her tiny frame on the back of a hog and slit its throat. Johnnie Ann was the strong matriarch in the family and one of the only women who didn't have a mental illness. She raised nearly a dozen of her own and her sister's children, including my mom, whom everyone called Margaret.

Mom's cousins said she floated into a room like a breeze, lingering without a sound before she would float back out. She liked school, but she wasn't great at it because she couldn't always get her brain to work the way most people could. All the way through high school and into junior college, she leaned on God.

If her real father wouldn't have her, she'd have a heavenly one. He was the only one that mattered. She did like boys too. But they always got her in trouble and disappeared when it came time to do something about that trouble.

The first time she got pregnant, she was so ashamed that she wore a girdle to keep it a secret. Her first son was born with cerebral palsy. She couldn't conceal him, but he grew anyway, and then she was faced with a decision: how was she going to care for him? She was barely out of her aunt's house, and she couldn't even figure out how to take care of herself. She was a smart secretary, great on the phone, excellent at finding help. Resourceful. She found a home for him far away in rural Pennsylvania. She made it out there to visit Leonard about once a year. Marguerite had three more babies with Carlos, her only husband. No sooner than the last one was born, they were divorced.

I only know this much of my mom's story because of my big sister, Rita. Rita was Mom's oldest daughter. She was born with vitiligo—her skin is a brown-and-white map of the world, islands around her wide, sweet smile. My brother Manny was born talking as fast as he walked, always darting around, his brow furrowed. And then there was Jose, a boisterous kid who collected fireflies and promised he would grow up to take care of Marguerite because she needed protecting.

She was content to stop with Jose, even though having babies around made her feel needed, like she would never feel that loneliness she had felt when her mother died. And then the Lord took her twelve-year-old baby.

Marguerite never told anybody about how she got the news on the day that Jose died. Manny was on the bus, so maybe he was the one who told her. I know the story from asking Rita, Manny, and the lawyer that my mother hired to help her sue the city of Philadelphia for Jose's wrongful death. The lawyer gave me the most details.

Jose was on his way to school on a city bus. When a group of kids jumped off, he did too—they were going to get candy from a store a few stops away from school. Then he changed his mind and turned back. When he tried to hop back on, the driver didn't see that Jose wasn't fully on the bus. Manny said he and a bunch of other kids tried to yell at the driver, get his attention, get him to stop, but the driver took off, and the bus wheels rolled over Jose's chest.

Marguerite's baby boy died at the scene. The life she had built up until 1976 died with him. Before Jose's death, she kept her kids clothed and fed and went to work every day. After her baby was gone, she stopped going to work and paying bills and hardly bought food. Her mother was dead, her baby was dead, and she did not want to talk to a therapist, a priest, or anybody else about it. What was there to say?

The result was that whatever parts of her bipolar and border-line personality disorders had been latent began to emerge. She would talk incessantly at times, disappear for long stretches with various lovers and, randomly slip into violent, abusive rages fairly often. She would beat and hurl insults at her children until they curled up in a bed out of her sight and wept.

It got to be so unbearable that Manny left when he was fifteen, leaving Rita behind. At the time, Johnnie Ann had a restaurant on the Jersey Shore, so he went there to work and didn't look back. When Mom finally started working again, she met Victor, a tall, re-served army vet who favored Barry White in demeanor and girth. Her boss asked her to walk the newly divorced engineer from one building to another in Center City. He told her that he mostly kept to himself because he had grown up with eight siblings in Alabama. She knew a little about growing up in a house full of kids.

They gambled together some weekends and made love after the high of winning or the frustration of losing had worn off, and next thing they knew, Marguerite was pregnant. She thought it was a miracle, God had taken her baby but had given her a new one: me. One of her neighbors had a little girl named Shonda, and because I was born about a year after Jose died, she blended Jose with Shonda. As much as I love my name and its meaning, it took a while for me to grow into it, to get comfortable carrying Jose's legacy with me as I strive to make my own.

Rita stayed to help take care of me. We moved to Chester, a Philadelphia suburb. Marguerite bought the little two-story house with settlement money she got from suing the city for Jose's death. The amount of money she got was substantial, but it did not make her rich and it would not last forever, especially not the way that she spent it. She favored taking off for weeks at a time to paying the mortgage or buying groceries for Rita and me.

Rita would look after me when my mother was gone, a hero who stepped in to do the work of a mother even when our mom was right in front of us. Once, on a trip down south to visit my mom's relatives in Orangeburg, South Carolina, when I was an infant, Rita said that we were all in a car and I was riding in her lap. Somehow, the car door flew open and I ended up on the road. When they stopped the car, Rita was the one who came to get me. "You were just laying in the road like nothing had happened," she said, still impressed all these years later.

For some of her teenage years, Rita stayed to help my mother raise me, but she vowed to leave as soon as she graduated high school. Mom's temper was unpredictable, and it took little or no provocation for her to hit or punch Rita during the random outbursts that had started after Jose died.

Rita left Mom's house when she was seventeen. She went to foster care before my great aunt Johnnie Ann took her in. When Rita left, Johnnie Ann told me later, she figured that Marguerite had lost all of her other children, so she didn't have the heart to try and rescue me from the chaos that was going to unfold later on. My family decided to leave me with her and pray for the best.

It took me a lot of wandering, therapy, and prayer to forgive my family for what felt like total abandonment when I learned the full story as an adult. I came to understand that self-preservation means exactly that—not everyone can be rescued. But my inner child was wounded and hurt beyond logic, in a way that took years to truly heal.

⊷⊷

One of the first things I learned from Marguerite is that the death of a child warps a mother's desire to live in the world. We live now in a time where this abnormality has been conveyed as a rite of passage for black mothers who abruptly lose their sons and daughters—often in police custody or at the hands of law enforcement. This has become so pervasive that it sometimes feels like an anomaly for black people to live and to live well.

But before there was a Black Lives Matter movement, I had witnessed firsthand through my mother's life that losing a child could open up a canyon in your spirit and heart that might make it difficult for anyone to ever really reach you again. There was a kind of defeat that sank into my mother's flesh that other mothers who had not lost children did not seem to experience. She could love me with her words, but her actions, along with her emotional presence, were always elusive.

I experienced my mother from this emotional distance my entire life, but when I was young, I had never had any validation of it from someone who understood psychology and how the brain works. When I was in my twenties and living in Oakland, a therapist with a medical organization for low-income seniors where my mother had gone at some point for evaluation called to explain what I had failed to understand for so long.

He asked me a series of questions—had my mother been abusive without reason that I could understand? Was she often inconsolable afterward? Each question resonated with me, and I began to feel that, finally, someone else could see more clearly the life I had lived with her that had caused me to flee.

When he was done with his questions, the counselor told me that he thought Marguerite had either bipolar disorder or borderline personality disorder. It wasn't until six months before her death, when I was the closest to her that I would ever be, that I had the courage to investigate what living with that dual diagnosis meant.

Her untreated, unmedicated mental illnesses explained why and how she could talk *at* me for thirty years while I listened—frustrated, confused, and exhausted. They explained her reckless spending and deep narcissism and her inability to keep a checking account or save any money, which meant that we were always lurching from one financial emergency to another. It was her broken relationship to money that fueled our frequent evictions from apartments throughout New York City when I was a child, and the evictions that she faced alone when I finally escaped the madness we lived through together.

Her bipolar diagnosis also explained her restlessness, why she felt so high and wealthy one moment that she needed to shout about it and, without warning, how she could drop so low into dark valleys that caused her to lament and despair.

She might grab a broom to swing against my body like a bat until she exhausted herself if something triggered a mood. Minutes later, she would plead aloud to Jesus to forgive her as she wept. Another gift my mother gave me was the gift of faith, and it was my belief in God, however fragile at the beginning, that helped me cope with deep confusion and sadness.

Faith was the one thing my mother was consistent about. Some things were shaped by her insanity, but I never believed that her faith in God was one of them, in part because we survived whatever chaos befell us.

Yet there was a gap between us and no bridge could cross it, not even Jesus. Even when she was physically present, her mind, her thoughts, and her dreams were somewhere else. It was as if I grew up with a stranger, a ghost. This was the hardest thing about my young life, in part because it is an unusual way to for one's life to begin with a mother who is living.

For the first fifteen years of my life, Mom was an enigma. Even when I was too young to care for myself, she left me alone for hours at a time, probably because she couldn't afford child care. While she was away, she would call from a pay phone on her walk back from wherever she had gone—from Brookhaven, she would sometimes walk to Philadelphia to get carfare and money from the Catholic Charities office; she might walk from the Bronx to Manhattan or something similar and do the same thing. Our conversations were not so much a back and forth as an opportunity for her explain what she planned to do each day in long, unfiltered monologues. Often, there was no having a conversation with Marguerite. She would talk for ten minutes straight, breathless, and I would talk for one.

"I know there's no food in the fridge, baby, I'm so sorry. Mommy loves you. I have to call the social worker and ask her about my check, it wasn't as big as the last time, and I don't know why they don't give us more. I think we just need to wait another five days, and then we'll have food stamps and cash and everything, OK? We're going to live it up, right?" She would laugh, not exactly nervous but also not really waiting for me to say anything. I would answer yes even though I didn't think living it up had anything to do with food stamps or welfare money.

"I love you, Shan. I love you more than I love myself. I know things are hard now, but your mom is working things out. I'm going to see you in a few hours. I have to run a few more errands, and then I'll be able to come back home."

Few things unraveled me like my mother's rages. Maybe it seems pat and melodramatic to describe her this way, but when she got spun up in a fit, she behaved like the Hulk. There was never any telling what might set her off—psychologists describe it best as walking on eggshells. We would be sitting in separate rooms, and the next thing I knew, my mother would be pacing, breathing heavily, tossing things, grabbing my flesh, smacking, punching, sweating, and screaming. It was one thing to watch after-school specials or sitcoms that explored child abuse, but it was something else to experience it at the hands of someone who could not control her anger.

I was always left confused, devastated, hurt, and ashamed. I could never figure out what I had done wrong, except for being in the room when she happened to have a manic episode. Without any context about her mental state, without knowing what I would be looking for to learn more about, I grew up in a constant state of fear, always trying to prepare myself for my mother to pounce, to steel my body against whatever attack might come at any moment. I believe the term for this now is *toxic stress*. At the time, it just felt like the world I was born into.

There was no confronting her about these things, either. Marguerite did not acknowledge anything she didn't want to hear, which was 90 percent of whatever any of her children (or anyone else) said to her. Being her daughter was like growing up with a big sister who stayed out partying, came home to sleep for a few hours, and never told you her plans or what she did. I knew that she was supposed to be taking care of me, but nothing in our lives unfolded the way I thought it was supposed to based on what I knew of the lives of our neighbors or people I saw on television.

I was born an introvert, and as the only remaining child of a single mother with mental illnesses, I moved even deeper into myself, folding in all my thoughts about being a burden to my mother and internalizing the belief that without me, she probably could have had the freedom she really wanted. I did not think I was cute or enough. I thought I was smart only because I was obsessed with reading. Otherwise, I thought that I kind of sucked as a replacement kid.

Of course, it wasn't that simple. Nothing ever is.

At the core of my confusion about my mother had always been her rage, manifested in manic episodes that began with ranting about her exhaustion with the world, with *this shit*. She had had enough. Why was everything so hard?

She would linger there, like she was warming up, tossing out rhetorical questions until she got to statements about how she couldn't wait for God to take her away from this place to his kingdom. She couldn't wait to go be with her heavenly father. I don't remember exactly when in this time period her rage would be directed at me or how I became a part of what agitated her. But there was always a clear shift of my mother from someone who knew I was her baby girl to someone who didn't seem to hear me when I pleaded with her to stop hitting me or respond when I touched her fleshy upper arm to ask if she was OK.

Reading, then writing, became my only freedom from the confusion these episodes sparked. No one from my family was really around for me to talk to about them, to ask if they were just a regular part of how she was or not. So I read to escape. I wrote. I prayed to a God I wasn't particularly sure about to make it clear to me why I shouldn't kill myself...because the idea of dying seemed more peaceful than the life I was living.

At the end of my mother's life, I was the reluctant guardian of these memories. I was reluctant because I wanted our story to be different. Years ago, at a meditation retreat, I'd heard someone say that forgiveness was giving up all hope for a better past. Wanting a different story is a nicer way of saying I did not want to forgive her. Ultimately, I feared that refusing to do so would put me at risk for a kind of bitterness I did not want in my life, where my mother haunted me in a perpetual manic state for the rest of my days because I just would not forgive.

At the time I was still meditating, or at least trying. I sat in meditation and prayer, trying to retrace our brief moments of joy. I remembered her declaring us rich because she got a check for $1,000. Her eyes got wide and she grabbed my hand to pull me onto the subway so we could hurry up to cash it and go from store to store buying things until all the money was gone. She thought I was a genius and said as much, far more often than she berated me or made me feel unwanted by calling me a bitch. That was how I learned the power of words, fantasies, and dreams.

You are not your mother. This is what therapist after therapist repeated to me. I needed the reminder, because I believed we were the same. My mother's borderline personality disorder enmeshed us with each other. She said it was because she breastfed me that I seemed to absorb everything she was experiencing, as if it were happening to me. "We have a connection; we have this bond," she would say. "God gave it to us."

She kept herself from loneliness by making me her mirror, a container for her emotions. She also inserted herself into any and all efforts I made to be an individual, which was central to my work as a writer. By nature, I was far more reserved than she, with no curves to speak of as a thin child, so it felt safe to button up the men's shirts I picked from the thrift store. Mom would unbutton the first button or two and tell me it looked like I was choking. *Be more like me*, the gesture seemed to say. *Get loose.*

When I had nice things, which wasn't often when we lived together, she would get jealous and, like any hater you've ever known, she would launch into sabotage mode. I once bought a beautiful taupe, navy, and burgundy ankle-length cotton dress—it had a kind of handkerchief print, the kind you might buy at a festival. "You look so beautiful in that, Shan," she said, gasping. Days later, while I was out, I came home to find the dress on my bed, the seams at the waist busted out on either side from my mother's bulbous belly because she'd tried it on with what she thought was our shared body instead of her separate one. I knew she hadn't intended to ruin my dress, but I couldn't understand why she couldn't let me have this one pretty thing for myself.

Whenever I expressed negative emotions, whether it was sadness or anger, Mom would tell me not to do it, as if by crying or being mad, I was somehow threatening her happiness. When I thought about it, I realized that the emotions of other people—mainly me, because I was the only person who was around her most of the time—must have made her feel like she had to live in the real world and she never really wanted to.

If I told her I was upset about something, she became dismissive and irritated. For most of my childhood, she might even stutter a little when people were emotional around her, though she worked on her stutter so that it didn't come up as much when I grew older. It was as if tears were her enemy, a sign of the weaknesses that made her feel more vulnerable. "Don't you cry," she would say. "Don't you do it."

That was only a tall order because everything in my life felt like something to cry about. I did, eventually, learn to keep my feelings to myself. Sort of.

Over the years, I would let my emotions out in all kinds of ways—on paper, with friends, inappropriately when I got bullied and I kicked a locker or tried to kill myself with a bottle of Ibuprofen (it was a cry for help more than a permanent solution, but I didn't even bleed or pass out or anything, which I thought was frustrating, funny, and maybe God's way of keeping me alive all at once).

As a kid, I slept a lot. When I got older, I slept around a lot. I was addicted to men and women and sex and the idea of love... and my warped understanding of what love and romance were supposed to be. I drank and smoked too much, trying to self-destruct because I was in so much emotional pain and I was so lonely that I just wanted someone to see how lonely I was, how much I needed a mother. I was not particularly ashamed to be a poster child for the crazy shit that can happen when you don't have a mother.

At the same time, I have always had an internal compass pointed north. When Rita was off on her own and I was not sure if God had forgotten me, I became my own North Star. My own hero. I give credit to God, my ancestors, the spirit of my brother, and luck for this.

Because the thing is, my shame related to my mother was not just that I felt I didn't have a mother. It was that I had a mother who was not able to take care of me because she could barely take care of herself. I had to try to take care of both of us...until I couldn't.

It was not until the end of her life that I ever began to consider that the two of us were lonely orphans. Each of us was lonely in our own particular way. Not only did I feel abandoned by her inability to care for herself or me, now I could see that the final abandonment was coming. I would have to bear our shared loneliness alone. Life was not fucking fair. It had never been fair to us, and it was not being fair to us now.

Three, maybe four times, I had therapists who shook their heads when I would promise them that growing up in more than a dozen shelters, welfare hotels, subsidized apartments, and halfway houses with my crazy mother had also made me crazy. *You are not your mother*, they all repeated.

But...but...I had her reddish-brown skin, her high cheekbones, her bright smile and full lips, and her broad forehead. Everything else was courtesy of Victor, but I was definitely Marguerite's child. Looking in the mirror, I saw her face increasingly as I got older. I had to move away to discover that my identity could be separate— that it was *supposed to be* separate.

Even when I left her house as a teenager to go to boarding school, I was still convinced that I was too much like her to have my own life or any version of freedom. That I loved, worshipped, and loathed her only made things more complicated.

And then, at the end of summer of 2011, Rita said Mom was missing. This was the only indication we had that something was wrong after two weeks of not hearing from her.

Weekly, sometimes daily, Mom would call one of her children. What bonded us across state lines was complaining that she liked to call us before the sun came up. "As soon as I get some monies, I'm going to send you some and then I'm going to sue this stupid city to build my Bible bookstore that my father in heaven told me in a dream he wants me to have," she would say.

Rita's relationship with Mom was complicated too, but there has only ever been love between me and Rita. I love her with the deep affection soldiers who have served in battle must feel, the loyalty, admiration, and appreciation you have for people who know how you've fought to stay alive. I loved her even before I knew why she left home and why she left me behind. Once she was gone, she told me years later, Mom refused to let her visit us at the house in Brookhaven, where we sometimes went without food or running water for days.

The little girl in me once wished that Rita had stayed with me. I know she survived our childhood by leaving and that she had to take care of herself. But until Mom got sick, a small part of me was still hurt, angry, and envious that Rita escaped. I knew if she had taken me with her, my life would have been so different, so much better. But I also know she couldn't have. She was just a kid. Later, she would explain tenderly, "I wanted to be there for you, but I thought I would kill Mom if I stayed."

I was also just a baby. Mom's last one. So I grew up fending for myself in the house of a madwoman, with and without a family. I grew up missing my sister and knowing my brothers without knowing anything about them beyond what Mom told me, which wasn't very much. I knew where they lived. I would see them every now and then, but it was like visiting a museum because of the emotional distance. They belonged to someone else, not me, and I did not know why until years later. If they had survived without me, I would survive without them.

It was just like being an orphan.

Rita built bridges—she did it as a missionary and in her youth ministry at church, and she did it with me. Even though we didn't grow up in the same house, Rita would find me wherever Mom and I were. She visited first in the early 1990s, before I graduated middle school. Mom reluctantly told my sister where she was, and Rita came to tell me she was going to the mission field abroad and that she would be gone for as long as God wanted her over there.

Whenever I started to doubt God, my sister popped up somewhere. Even when she and my brother-in-law were missionaries, she and I stayed connected online. She was my first pen pal, back in the days of screeching and slow dial-up modems. Rita e-mailed to remind me that God loved me and that I should keep going. She flew from halfway across the world to be at my high school and college graduations. *Look*, her actions said. *I'm your sister, I love you, and I will always show up for you.*

She loved me around Marguerite's massive presence and despite her absences and then, around the eclipse that was Mom's cancer. Before Mom got sick, I would call Rita every now and then, at my mother's provocation, but stop when I was smoking or drinking or doing anything I thought she might disapprove of. I resented that she had a daughter whom I was supposed to love as my niece but who took her attention away from me. I was jealous that she had a life that I craved—stability and familial love—and I hated myself for my jealousy, for being petty like Mom could be.

I was feeling all of that when Rita called in 2011 to tell me that Mom was missing.

"Have you heard from her?"

"No," I said.

Rita was rattled, like Manny. Johnnie Ann was worried, too.

There was no answer at Mom's door in Philly, and she was not picking up the phone.

Her voicemail was full. *You have reached…leave a message and I will call you at my earliest convenience* every day for seven, eight, nine days. On the eleventh day, Rita and my niece knocked on the door again. They found a landlord with a key to let them in to the house. Mom was emaciated, the house filled with the scent of urine and feces, dust, and darkness.

"She hadn't had anything to drink or eat for weeks, so we called the ambulance," Rita said.

"She was trying to kill herself," I said.

Rita paused. "I think so. She said something to me about cancer."

I stared at some of the mail Mom had sent as I sat in my home office, a stack of worn manila envelopes with red felt-tip pen markings on the front. Instead of her full name above her address, she had simply written Mom. Next to my name, she'd put in quotes, "My baby girl." I'd hastily opened them with decreasing glimmers of hope that maybe they would make sense, but over the years, they were more and more confusing and cryptic, sometimes with palms or plastic rosaries or Catholic calendars enclosed.

If Marguerite was dying, I was going to kill my entire life. Cancer was too much. The thought of it, the sound of it, filled me with so much emotion that I felt assaulted by anything like normal life. I could not have a conversation about the weather or think about food or watch the sun rise or set without thinking, *My mother is dying and I don't know how long she has left.*

After a decade as a newspaper reporter, I left the only career I had known as an adult. I stopped going out. I had run two other marathons after New York, but I could barely run anymore. After working three jobs and going to grad school while working full time and freelancing and pitching books to agents and getting scores of rejection letters, I was burned out.

Now, my mother was ready to die and I was about done with life too. I was tired. I started drinking and smoking again. I just wanted to be in my house with my dog, Cleo. If Mom was giving up, I wanted to give up too. I felt I reserved the right to die selfishly just like she and my father did.

My whole life my mother had withheld herself from me because no one had taught her that when you love a child, you hold her and hug her instead of just talking to her about love. Now, she would be gone forever. I couldn't answer for myself the question of whether or not that was something she truly wanted.

She had failed in a dozen ways with five different children and so many lovers, clinging instead of loving, my life her raft back to a shore resembling normal. "I'm not *old* old," she'd said when I'd asked for her exact age. For a stretch of time in the 1990s, she celebrated her fortieth birthday for several years in a row each Labor Day. It was a small thing but still a thing a girl should know about her mother. She kept things like that a secret from me for no reason at all.

So my worry, despair, compassion, and rage, my sympathy, defensiveness, and sadness about the end of her life made a throbbing, multilayered knot of heat in my chest. Would I be free of it once she was gone, or would it haunt me forever?

I had time—but not much—to consider it as Mom lay in the cool darkness of a Philly nursing home room that stank of stale urine and apple juice. Her wide brown eyes, with slivers of turquoise at the edges of her pupils, stared into an invisible abyss beyond me and the television, hovering near the ceiling, waiting to fall into a void. In less than six months, she would be gone.

I fell into a chair and put my forehead against her shriveled hand. She felt my tears on her skin and said, weakly, "Don't do that. Don't cry."

I couldn't stop the tears once they started. It was too much to see her like this. Defeated. In limbo. The past she fled behind her now. She was dying in an institution just like her mother. She was dying, and I worried that I still needed her—that if she could survive this, she could really be my mother.

The little girl in me had hoped one day that the permanent fog of crazy would lift and God would give me a real mother, a woman who could tell me how much to save for retirement, how to cope with heartbreak instead spiraling into self-destruction, and how to keep my bones strong as an old lady. Lapsed Catholic and failing Christian that I have always been, I held out secret hope for my mother's eventual resurrection. Without realizing it, I had prayed for decades that I would get to have a biological mother who could care for both herself and me in my lifetime. I was mourning that woman at Mom's beside, crying about a life I wouldn't know how to define without her and desperately, endlessly sad about the life she would never get to have because hard living had finally taken over her flesh.

She had always filled up the room with her words, but now she was weak from medicine and from arguing with the nurses about wanting to go back to her things in the Section 8 house. These glimpses of her previous fire took me back to the old days. I thought of when she had actually stood up for me, and one memory stood out from the rest: the thrill of watching her tell off my first-grade teacher, Ms. Hines.

Back then, Mom was thick and sassy, her attitude defiant. She would not allow my first days as a student to deter me from being as stubborn or wild as she wished she had been. After Ms. Hines said something mean to me about smelling like urine (which I certainly did because I was a chronic bed wetter) my mother blessed her out on the elementary school steps.

"Who are you to talk about anybody looking like you do?" my mother demanded.

Ms. Hines was smoking a Newport. She had watery eyes that were brown like those of a fish and a juicy Jheri curl.

"She peed in class," Ms. Hines said, her voice a hiss. I remember standing almost behind Mom, too tall to grab her tree-trunk legs, but I felt like I should hold some part of her body in case she went flying in my teacher's direction.

"I don't care if she peed on your desk," Mom responded. "This is my child. It is your job to teach her, not to be mean to her. Don't make me come back here."

Don't make me come back here.

At thirty-three, I still wondered who would defend me when she was gone. The broader question was who I would belong to now that she was leaving me. It seemed out of the question that I would only belong to myself, which is exactly what freedom is. I shook my head and tears kept falling.

She wore a thin turquoise polyester scarf because the wig she'd worn every day became a matted mess when she'd locked herself in her house to die. Her salt-colored hair was cropped low, which she hated. My mother was a huge fan of long hair—she considered it a woman's glory.

A salmon-colored button-down blouse with a black hoodie kept her now-skinny body warm. She was less than half the size I remembered. I first noticed the weight loss in her hands. The fists my body remembered as heavy as bricks were now fragile doorknobs pressing against her thin skin from the inside. They had had so much flesh, so much life, even if it was life that scared me and scarred me and made me leave her like everyone else had. As I held her thin hands, I felt her pulse beating in her hand like a frightened bird.

Maybe she never really had a chance at the light of freedom. But she had at least been so strong, so powerful, once. Is this what God did to those who loved Him?

"I'm scared, Shan," Mom said.

"Me too," I said.

"I'm so glad you came to see me. You look great. You look like a model. My leg is really bothering me," she said, her brow furrowed like a worried child. "Don't look at my mouth. My teeth are all messed up. I still want to get them fixed." Her bottom teeth rose like a crown of ivory cutting into her top lip. "I'm sorry I'm sick," she added.

"You don't have to be sorry. Who cares about your teeth?"

Her laugh was nervous, soft, and staccato. The breathy laugh of a weary woman. The doctors would try to do MRIs and see her insides to see how far and fast the cancer had spread, and she would have none of it. For once, she was going to get to freedom.

She was going to die the way she had lived.

Finally.

CHAPTER 3

ALWAYS THINK ON YOUR FEET

Whenshe was younger, Marguerite rose quietly each morning before the sun came up. The silver Catholic medals of
the Virgin Mary, St. Joseph, and St. Christopher that she pinned
to the inside of her bra would chime against the metal of a large
safety pin. Once she stood on her feet, she wouldn't quit moving
until it was ten or eleven o'clock at night.

In a pre-Internet era, my mother had the kind of daily agenda
that would overwhelm even today's interconnected smartphone
geeks. She said her rosary first: her Hail Marys and Our Fathers
connected her to God and the angels she would refer to throughout the day. She told me all the time that she prayed for her children, but I imagine that she must have also prayed for money and
love. Once, she told me that she had considered becoming a nun
when she was first confirmed as a Catholic at eighteen. It turned
out she had the conviction and the fever for God that it would
take but not the discipline. "I guess God wanted me for something
else," she said.

Something else. This was how Marguerite described things when
she was bemused and when she was not sure what else to say. She
was something else as a single mom, as a woman. Her clothes always

hugged her muffin top, and there was always more lipstick on her teeth than her lips. She stomped through the world more than she sauntered, her shoulders a bit hunched over time, but always back, chest high.

The only way you might guess she wasn't as confident as she seemed was if you caught her in a lie or asked her where she was from. When we first moved to New York, mom would start to stutter, and impatient strangers made it hard for her to finish her sentences as she tapped her foot hard against concrete to force her words out. Even when she was stuttering, she used the same outside voice she used to sing at the top of her lungs from the first pew at church to shout her answers at people.

She was something else, though I would have preferred for her to be like everybody else—a quiet chameleon instead of a rainbow-clad lightning storm of a woman, drawing eyes to us everywhere we went. Even her feet, thick with callouses and corns, were something else. When she walked, the floor beneath us shook as she thumped her way around. Her footfall always seemed to signal a warning drumbeat. It was how she walked around the house in Brookhaven, through the sidewalks of our little suburb and onto Greyhound buses in and out of state.

We never went anywhere quietly or easily, and we rarely fit in anywhere because we were always moving. Sometimes, the law intervened and separated us.

More than thirty years later, I only vaguely remember having a run-in with my mother and a hot straightening comb. I don't remember if it was my fault for squirming away from the steaming hot comb straight from the stove pilot or if Mom burned me with it on purpose, but I do remember the comb searing into the flesh of my arm. I wailed like a siren.

"Stop that screaming!" Mom said over my shouting, stomping over to the refrigerator to put pats of butter on her fingertips and smear them on the burn, which turned a dull blue-black like the eyes of a fly. I would not stop screaming because it hurt. Not only was I burning, I remember feeling for the first time like I was not safe. I was not safe in that moment or in that house or with her, and I hollered for my young life. When she burned me, I also understood why my siblings had left. I felt trapped in that house, stuck with her and like I was never going to get to leave like the others I barely knew.

It also made me wonder if she'd hurt me on purpose. The mothers and daughters I watched on television touched each other softly, with affection. There were no smoke plumes or fiery iron combs between them.

My screams startled the neighbors, who called the police. The cops called social workers with child welfare, who eventually came back to take me away for about a year.

It was the first and only time that I was separated from my mother as a girl. She had pretty much been my whole world up until that point, because we didn't really socialize with any of our neighbors and I had not yet been to school. I knew my mother, and I knew the inside of our house. I knew constant hunger—long stretches of days when I distracted myself with television because all we had to eat were carrots or canned meat from food pantries leftover from the last time my mother ran out of money to buy food—and I knew long silences when she left me alone and went out into the world.

But I did not know how to talk to people or ask for things. I was a feral, shy, skinny kid who was used to the water or the lights being cut off at any time. At the house in Brookhaven, at least, I figured if something really bad happened, my sister or brother would eventually be able to find me. In foster care, I didn't know where any of my relatives were or if they could have helped. Who would have told them to call Mom because her baby was with the authorities? Rita was the first face that flashed into my little girl brain, but…what was her number? I had no clue. Mom had forbidden her to visit or call or write. When most kids were learning how to ride bikes, I was wondering if I might ever see my mother again.

Most stories you hear about foster care are terrifying and stark and jarring, but it was nice at first. There was a structure to things. I didn't have to wait hours or days to eat like I did with Mom. There was always an adult around, and that felt odd—but nice. I felt protected.

It didn't take long for me to miss Mom. I lived with an older woman who was in a wheelchair somewhere in Philadelphia, in a house with two other children. She fed us Swanson frozen dinners with added sugar—but at least she fed us. A few months later, I was sent to live with a black couple in a wealthier suburb than the one I knew best. This couple had another daughter. She did not like me, and I did not like her. When my foster mother took us to buy bikes at Sears, I remember frowning at the demand that I pick out a pink bike.

"Blue is my favorite color," I said. "I'd like the blue bike." I was staring at one that had Batman on it. That was the one I wanted. The stubborn tomboy in me was strong.

My foster mom's face completely changed from excitement to do something nice for her real kid and her temporary one to absolute authority. "Blue is a boy color," she said.

I was silent. I did not talk back to adults, certainly not anyone who was acting in the capacity of my mother. I never wanted to find out what my mother would turn into if I talked back to her, questioned her, or even asked questions about any of her decisions.

My foster mom said, "You will get a pink bike, or I won't get you a bike."

I shook my head. "That's OK. Thank you."

She grumbled for a bit and then shook it off. At least with my crazy mother, I knew never to expect to have any kind of choice. Normal was a lot more work. It was not a balm—not for the burn on my arm or my nervous heart or for anything else. Five years was long enough for me to get used to upheaval, change, and chaos. That's what I returned to when Mom regained custody of me.

I remember walking into the house with her, thinking it looked like squatters had just left before we walked in. The renters she had met in the court system in Philly had essentially turned into just that, since they stopped sending rent payments toward the end of whatever agreement they had made with my mother.

Everything sagged—the couch, the curtains—in a way that it hadn't before. One of the kitchen windows was broken, which let in a stiff breeze. Mom looked around, walking slowly along the dirty, spinach-colored carpet before she paused at the stairwell and looked up into the darkness.

"Let's go, Shan," she said, turning on her heels and taking my hand as we left. She decided, just like that, that we were moving to New York City. It was the winter of 1984, and soon I would be six years old.

We had distant relatives in Harlem. She never explained who they were to us, how she had found them, or how long we would stay with them. I was too small to ask any questions. I was just relieved to be with her again, wandering. Even if life was harder with her, and I never knew when the next meal was coming, life with her was never dull.

No place gave her comfort, so I didn't relax either. I peed the bed so often it became part of my identity. It was a frustrating nervous habit that would last well into my teenage years.

I was skinny with messy braids, and I was always peeing and smelling like pee. I prayed that God would calm me down and fix the part of my brain that was so nervous that I couldn't even sleep right without wetting myself. While I was waiting for an answer on that, I watched my mother worry that something she might do or say might get us hurt or worse. I had a big job, she said.

"God gave you to me for taking Jose. He always said when he grew up he was going to take care of me," she would say. If I was his replacement, then kid logic suggested that I needed to take care of her. I didn't understand the concept of growing up because it seemed like I was already grown. After all, my mother already needed someone to take care of her—I couldn't wait until or depend on growing up. I would try, even though I didn't know what the hell that meant or how I was supposed to do it.

⌖

In 1984, New York City felt like a grand wilderness of glass and tall towers adorned in bright lights. It felt like a flood of sensation that we waded into from what was a relatively small, provincial place. The endless groans of cars, buses, and trains everywhere felt like constant company. The dirt and exhaust smelled familiar, even if the crowds were totally foreign. I wanted to inhale the entire place and carry it with me everywhere I went, and I wanted my eyes to be bigger so that I could see as much of it as I could keep in my brain at once. Even though we were homeless, for the first time in my life I felt like I had found home.

Our family in Harlem consisted of an aunt and uncle who agreed to let us stay with them temporarily. They must have thought we meant to stay a week at most. We rode the humid D train to their high-rise apartment near 145th Street and St. Nicholas, my hip wedged next to Mom's on the packed subway while I stared at the waves of bodies around us, climbed the dirty steps to the street, and rode the elevator that smelled like Pine Sol up to the eightieth floor of their building. I had never been so high up in the sky before that the people below looked like fleas. I've never been a huge fan of heights, and I trace the specific brand of nausea I feel back to that time…looking down on the city from their apartment.

They seemed so old to me then that I couldn't even imagine how old they were. How many years did it take for the hair around your face to start falling out and turning that silver gray and for your body to stop working? My wheelchair-bound great aunt Claie had a soft round face, and her birthday was in January like mine. My great uncle Bea was tall and yellow, as I imagined Paul Bunyan to be. He towered over the three of us the same way their building loomed over Harlem.

I had a little girl's sense of time, which is to say I had no idea how much time passed. Mom and I were guests for long enough to see Uncle Bea's mother waste away in a room that smelled like Vick's VapoRub, plastic, and ear wax. His dying mother was too old to talk—another thing I couldn't even fathom. When she opened her mouth, it was shaped like the wide oval of an empty cave, and the only sounds that came out were the soft whispers of a creaky door swinging on a hinge deep inside. The adults wouldn't let me close to her, like I might catch death the way one catches a cold.

I slept in the living room with Mom on the thin pullout sofa bed or the couches that wore plastic covering most of the time. When the old lady died, I slept in her room because I needed the rubber sheet like she did. It seemed like we were only there for a couple of days and nights, but it was probably more than a week. We were just starting to get comfortable when they told Mom we needed to leave.

Because it was a building for old people, and we were obviously not a part of that crowd.

Because people were starting to notice the obviously younger woman and her child in a residence where there were no other children.

Because, Marguerite, you can't just show up with a kid and no job, no money, and no plan and expect us to take care of you.

⚔

When it came to thinking on her feet, Mom was a genius. I thought of her face as an oracle, and whenever anything shifted in my world, I looked there instantly for an answer. I could tell the wheels were spinning in her brain when she would start talking about suing somebody.

Jose's death had turned her into the most litigious human being I'd ever met. I figured she wouldn't threaten to sue her flesh and blood, but she would sue anybody else for anything. That's not even an exaggeration. In the years following the bus accident, she would go on to sue her employers, companies, and lawyers. Maybe she was fixated on the legal system because it felt like free money—like gambling, it just took a little longer to get a check.

Studying the law would have given her good reason to pick New York City in the early 1980s. In 1979, a landmark case, *Callahan v. Carey,* had given every homeless woman and child in New York City the legal right to shelter. Family homelessness, which had once been rare and the result of fires or natural disasters, spiked from an estimated 950 families sheltered by New York City in 1982 to more than 3,000 in 1984, the year we arrived. While at the time it felt like we were utterly alone, we were actually part of an unfortunate trend of families who were the faces of new urban poverty.

I took it personally, the way children do. I wondered if my aunt and uncle knew I had been stealing mail to get money. Back then, people still sent cash in the mail, and when I got lucky, when I could hold an envelope up to the light and check for the solid dark rectangle of a handsome stack of twenty-dollar bills, I would feel rich and like Jose would be proud of how I was taking care of me and Mom. Mom didn't ask any questions. When I told her I found the money, which was only half true, she would get wide-eyed and shout, "It's a miracle! Oh, Lord, thank you."

But I couldn't answer her big prayers, the ones about a place to stay and steady money. Mom stuttered through her words when her aunt told her we had to leave. That night. Couldn't we stay one more night?

No, they said. The landlord. The neighbors. It was too much.

I was anxious, afraid, and sad. I was angry at this conditional God who seemed to turn his back on us like our blood relatives who blinked at our hesitation like apathetic strangers. It was good, as a child, to learn that family could be worse than your worst enemy. I kept my eyes on the floor for a long while, looking up to watch Mom pull on our aunt's old fake mink coat and drop eight quarters into one of the pockets. I got Mom's old one, a thick tweed coat that hung on my small frame like a blazer on a hanger.

There was a family shelter across the bridge between Harlem and the Bronx, a walk of about ten or twelve blocks. The money was for carfare, but Mom opted for the harder way, as usual. It was a stark, cold night in mid-December, and cars weren't passing on the bridge. The streetlights hung over us in cones of copper light that barely shined bright enough to reflect on the still, black river below. We were breathing hard in the cold air, heads down, when two men approached us with a gun.

"Give us your money!" We hadn't heard their footsteps because of our breath, because even when it is quiet, New York City is loud. One of them pressed a gun to my head, my pulse beating in my ears as I held my breath and bit my lip. *I don't want to die, I don't want to die* was all I could think until I almost said: *Please don't kill my mother.*

I could see on her face that she was petrified. They must have thought the jacket real mink. As one of them yanked it from her body, the quarters in her pocket clanged against concrete.

"Oh my God," Mom shouted, until the man behind her covered her mouth. "I don't have any money," she said into his palm. I stood there, shaking. They took her purse, which had all our lives in it: a little bit of cash, social security cards, and birth certificates. "Please, don't shoot."

"Keep walking," the one with the gun said, and they ran off with our things as we stood in the cold winter night, faces wet, our chests rising and falling. Mom's breath formed white smoky clouds against the quiet blackness when they were gone, my shaking hand pressed in her sweaty palm. Now we knew why there were no other pedestrians on the bridge. We were alive at least, keeping each other warm with the fear in our blood, walking to safety.

⇌

Mayor Ed Koch thought the homelessness we were living would be temporary. He created the Emergency Assistance Unit, a three-room Manhattan way station for people who were always looking for shelter. It operated around the clock. He opened welfare hotels, or beds in hotels that were designated for the temporarily homeless, and eventually pieced together subsidized housing for people like us who couldn't live in shelters for too long without going a little crazy.

We first slept at the bottom of a high-ceiling gym in the Roberto Clemente family shelter that looked like a gutted factory. Hundreds of cots were lined up next to one another, like a warehouse being used as a triage unit. We lived there for weeks before we moved into a one-bedroom apartment on Burnside Avenue.

Finally, after a couple of years living in too many different places for me to register for school at the beginning of the actual school year, I got to enroll like a regular student again at P.S. 26. After school, Mom took night classes at Bronx Community College, so I went with her until we got evicted from the Burnside apartment. For someone so smart, she knew nothing about bills, or maybe she knew about them and just didn't care.

Instead of making our way to the EAU and another shelter, Mom changed course and we went back to Brookhaven the year I was in third grade. She went back to say goodbye to the house, which was near foreclosure, and to file for bankruptcy.

It helps me to remember the order of our frequent moves based on the outrageous things that happened during each one.

I was about nine years old, for instance, when Mom hauled me to a Harlem salon owned by a James Brown doppelganger who called himself Mister Tee. In a couple of years, there would be no surprise money in the form of the settlement checks. Mom spent it like it would be depleted sooner than that.

This was before weaves became standard fare for black women. Despite my mother's feelings on the matter, weaves would never be appropriate for children. Nevertheless, Mister Tee—who wore his hair in a slick coif, not a 'frohawk like the famous "A-Team" character—laid out lines of human hair layers that cost hundreds of dollars.

"What we got here?" he asked, sounding like one of my foster moms.

"What can you do?"

"What you want done?"

And on it went, until, after hours of pulling needle, thread, and layers of longer hair out of a wooden drawer, then sewing, stitching, pressing and curling, my skinny head sagged with the weight of new fake shiny curls. My scalp ached and there were strands of hair all over my shirt. The mirror revealed what my neck had already told me: I looked like a Chia Pet impersonating Diana Ross.

"You are beautiful," Mom said, smiling and showing off the gap between her front teeth. As usual, I had a feeling she was lying. The kids at the Toby Farms Elementary School confirmed that feeling. At the playground, some kid accused me of having a weave.

I am Marguerite's child—a horribly bad liar.

"It's mine! Look!" I tried to shake it and point to the sewn roots, but there was no point. They pointed, laughed, and tugged. Thankfully, I wouldn't be there for more than a month.

The rest of third grade was a blur. We returned to New York City, which was starting to feel more like home than Philly or Chester, even if we were firmly a part of the permanently homeless. We made the rounds, living at the Catherine Street Shelter in Lower Manhattan, motels in Times Square and Hell's Kitchen, and finally a halfway house in Harlem run by Ursuline nuns in light blue and white habits. There would be a few more places that would be ours and then snatched away. No matter where we were, Mom rose in the morning darkness before five a.m., pressed her hands together with rosary beads between her fingers, and prayed before plotting our next move.

CHAPTER 4
MASTER THE GAME

Marguerite loved the sound of money, and what money made possible, so I learned to love it too. Cash meant security and celebration. Money promised food and comfort.

Whatever the game is, money buys hope that you can win. When you've been hungry for days or coming up short of money to get on the train, finding a couple of dollars on the street feels like God wants you to be free and fed. Whole.

I did not play games much as a child. I was the kid who felt more at ease with adults. While girls my age frolicked and played black girl games, twisting their hips and playing Rockin' Robin, singing chants while slapping palms in a kind of coordinated dance that I never knew, I watched with slight pangs of jealousy. The same was true of little boys zipping past me on bikes or tumbling out of low tree branches.

That kind of fun made my heart beat too fast for my comfort, since I was clumsy and would fall and scrape my knee just from walking too fast and tripping over an uneven sidewalk. The physical pain was only part of the problem. I also never wanted to be seen.

When I wasn't talking and trying to befriend teachers, my mother, social workers, the people at Mass, I kept my head in a book. I liked the other outsiders, but we were all loners, out of step with the rest of humanity. It was that kind of introversion that made it easy to cope during Mom's gambling sprees in Atlantic City.

Marguerite chased money with wild-eyed glee. The only thing that might have made her happier than the settlement checks would have been Ed McMahon showing up at our door with a Publisher's Clearinghouse camera crew and an oversized check... that she would have spent in less than two weeks.

If I had known a therapist, or maybe if we had been in a community where people witnessed her patterns over time, my mother's fixation on money and inability to keep it in her grasp might have raised some flags. As it was, the direct result of her single-minded pursuit of cash when I was a kid was that she often left me for long stretches in arcades housed inside Atlantic City's casinos, where Manny worked.

Even with the last of her money, Mom would put us both on a Greyhound bus from Port Authority early on a Saturday before the sun was up. She would buy me dry orange cheese crackers filled with peanut butter for breakfast from the vending machines lining the walls before we filed into the cool, dark buses with the plush polyester seats.

Our Greyhound squealed to a stop at a tiny bus station in Atlantic City, which looked like an old parking lot. Compared to the towering, impressive skyline in New York, I always thought buildings in Atlantic City looked bootleg. The casinos and hotels looked like boxy bodies huddled in a corner near the sea.

Marguerite looked at those buildings as if they might change her destiny. She eyed them the same way she sized up handsome men she fawned over—like her favorites, Clint Eastwood and

Charles Bronson. The gleam in her eye matched the sun glinting from the dark glass.

If we were wealthy, she would have been called eccentric and whimsical. Manny had different opinions of my mother's gaming binges.

"You can't just show up whenever you want, Mom."

"I know, but I wanted to see you."

"You wanted to gamble," he said, adding, "You don't even have any money to gamble!"

Manny spoke in a strained whimper that sounded like a slowly deflating balloon, while Mom tried using her inside voice by talking in a loud whisper. He rarely cracked a smile. He usually had the popular haircut of his era, a fade or flat top.

We usually found him at work, typically a fine-dining establishment where he wore a white uniform so crisp it looked like it had never been worn before, impatience wrinkling his forehead. He had continued working in the service industry since his teenage years.

"You can't just be doin' this, Mom," he would whisper. Mom would fidget and say, "Shan is hungry. I'm hungry."

Although Manny had left her home as a teenager, Mom somehow sensed that he would never turn her away. He would fuss, but he would not let her struggle, and she would not let him refuse her. In a match of wills, Marguerite always won the game.

"How you doin', Shan?" Like Mom, he never called me by my full name; it was like all the letters were too much of a bother.

"OK," I would say back to him. Manny's permanent expression was one of worry. I always wanted to try to make him smile, but it always seemed to be beside the point.

He would usher us to a table while his coworkers stared.

I usually strained to keep my eyes on the Atlantic Ocean, unfurling before the Jersey Shore outside of windows so clean I could see the reflection of our bodies and an unfurling blanket of water crawling over sand at the same time.

Did he feel obligated to respond to Mom's crazy because he had been riding the bus that killed his little brother? Maybe it was because Mom was like a lot of other women—she loved her sons best as she could, though she could never be a father, so she hoped loving them would be instruction enough to show them how to grow into men while she concentrated everything she thought she knew about how to be a woman on raising her daughters.

When Manny fussed at Mom, he was telling her he would not play the game the way she wanted him to. When she whined back at him, or just said OK, she was telling him that she was going to win, she was going to get her way. I watched this dynamic both embarrassed and confused by my family.

Manny knew what Mom would order, and I usually ordered the same thing: a fried seafood combination with fries. While he was scribbling on his notepad, Mom said, "Manny, OK, I know...we're not going to be here that long and I brought you some monies."

"Stop saying that! You don't have money. Come on now. Look at you. The same thing happens whenever you come! You show up, you lose all your money, and then you need me to give you some for y'all to get home. And I can't afford it! I need this job! You can't just keep showing up like this. It's not right."

Aside from me, Manny was the only person in our extended family that Mom saw regularly. Manny and Rita were the only ones who complained when Mom just showed up. Rita didn't allow it under any circumstances and was usually not accessible by way of public transportation anyway.

"Oh, Manny, you're no fun," Mom would say, looking at me with a smile that managed to convey both guilt and glee. Manny and I exchanged helpless stares while she laughed in a nervous staccato. Those eyes of hers went from blank cluelessness to warm celebration, no matter what we thought of her facial expressions or her impulse to gamble or any other behavior generally considered unsuitable for a mother.

To outsiders, we must have looked confused about the weather. Mom usually dressed for spring, no matter the actual season, so I grew up doing the same. I was in seventh grade before I realized that socks weren't optional for most people the way they were for us. Mom only wore them without shoes.

She'd be in some tight rayon blouse and a skirt. I'd wear some baggy shirt falling over my sliver of a waist with itchy wool trousers. The baggier an outfit, the better, for me. I felt safe in heavy folds of cotton—covered and camouflaged. I wanted everything to feel that way, to deflect attention away from me, since the spinning energy of my mother drew stares and looks all the time, like we were walking around inside a spotlight.

"Well, I just wanted to see you," she'd pout.

"Call next time. They have phones in New York." He would look at me with that permanent fish mouth frown. We would both look down at my feet with open disapproval. His dark brown eyes with the tightly curled lashes I envied softened when he looked at me. *What could we do about our mother?*

When it was time for Mom to go to the casino at the entrance to the dark arcade, Mom handed me a plastic bucket filled with ten dollars in quarters and a five-dollar bill. If she had bothered to squat down to eye level, she might have noticed my face twitching from trying not to cry those first few times. Once we became regulars, I didn't even bother to feel anything about it, because I knew the drill: she said she would be back soon, but it could be two hours or it could be five.

Being inside Atlantic City casino arcades felt like being stuck against the hot bulb of one of those crane games where nothing could lift you out into the fresh air, even though my eyes had been trained and sharpened by the darkness in the rooms around those hot boxes of seductive light. Like some other games, the slippery cranes also happened to be a waste of quarters. I once spent about two dollars in change only to end up with a rough polyester-feathered duck wearing a plastic Def Leppard pin.

During our initial trips to Atlantic City, I became aware that hand-eye coordination was not one of my gifts. Instead, surrounded by glowing screens, I longed for a comfortable seat and a book. Like the other kids who'd been abandoned while their folks went off to gamble, I tried my hand at one game after another. I didn't like the themes: I did not want to beat people up; Donkey Kong wasn't that much fun; I didn't like shooting snakes or centipedes. The only games I could really enjoy were pinball machines and Ms. Pac-Man. Even sticking with those games, I went through my allotted quarters long before Mom was done gambling for the day.

There was some kind of arcade code where us kids babysat the boxy machines as much as they were babysitting us. Because there were no windows, it was impossible to tell how much time had passed. I ran out of quarters in about an hour and a half. Every time.

Mom was radiant when she had money. The more she had, the taller her gait. She would strut like a model down a runway through New York City streets, a new jet-black wig with a perfect curl over one eye like a movie star. Her reddish-brown skin glowed with a secret knowledge. You could see the cash glowing from the new fake leather pumps that hadn't yet been molded by her calloused feet. I didn't get as many fancy new things as she did, but I got something better—chocolate and new books.

Still, I was usually one of the first kids dropped off in the arcade and the last to leave. It'd be me and some fake-ass security guard. When things got weird, which didn't take long, I would walk out of the arcade to guess what time it might be by looking out of the window and watching the waves until my Mom came back. I usually just wanted to sleep or eat, but without any money, I couldn't. Once or twice, she left me at the arcade for so long that I paged her from one of the beige hallway phones.

"I was winning! I can't believe it. I was on a roll and you inter-rupted," she said in one breath on the phone.

"It's been five hours," I said. "I don't have any quarters left."

"Fine. I'll come get you."

She did, but only after another hour. The game was more im-portant than me. It offered her something I couldn't—a chance at things she really wanted and an alternate reality where anything was really possible. But in real life, we were just ordinary poor black women. I was the only one who seemed to understand this.

I could tell by how Mom walked when she came to get me if she'd won or lost. If she had won any amount of money between thirty and a hundred dollars, Marguerite trotted with the fresh high of winning flushing her cheeks. When she lost, she walked like she had a limp and her head hung low like a dying sunflower. More often than not, we would end up at Manny's apartment after all our hours and money had been wasted, our sides touching on his sagging leather couch.

Mom stared out of a sliding glass door at the Atlantic, which appeared to roll right up to the window, in spite of the smaller houses and apartment buildings and the faded brown line of the boardwalk under the darkening sky. Manny's place smelled like Old Spice and strong, musky cologne and Chinese food.

"Ma, why do you always do this, spending all that money? I can't afford to do this, Ma, I can't. Not every time you just show up without calling."

"Oh, Manny..." Mom said.

Until I lived in one place for long enough to make a real friend, sometime during middle school, I didn't realize that normal peo-ple don't just show up places unannounced. They certainly don't do it without having any money. This was a recurring feature of Mom's mental illness, an aspect of her quirky personality that of-fered me a little bit of adventure to look forward to—and it was freeing and exciting, until someone like Manny balked, protested, mentioned how not fun it was for him or her.

Manny was the most generous man I knew as a child. He would give me whatever he had. He would tell me to take care of myself, to look after Mom, to call him if I needed anything. I would say OK, but I never called him when I needed something—because I always needed something, and I didn't trust anyone in my family to do anything about it.

When Mom was out of earshot, or in the bathroom, he would look at me and say, "You doing OK, sweetheart? I love you, man. I don't mean to fuss all the time, but Mom gotta do better. You need some shoes? I got some boots, man. Come on. Let me see if these will fit you. You got some big-ass feet."

Manny was surrounded by women who always needed something—I think this must have been why he gave us all the same Christmas gift year after year: perfume gift sets. Being a poor kid means being accustomed to already-used things, so I was always grateful to have something pretty, pink, and new. (Blue would remain my favorite color, bike or no, but as I grew older I became less of a tomboy in most ways.) In those boxes would be decadent, rich lotions that felt like silk on my skin and perfume that I always waited once or twice a month to spray on my thin wrists or behind my knees.

In contrast, Mom doused herself in the stuff, bathed in it like it was holy water; she flicked sprinkled perfume generously behind her ears and all over her forearms—nothing in moderation. I think something about smelling sweet made her feel womanly and wealthy. She is the reason I love Chanel perfume and scented lotion: after Mass at St. Patrick's Cathedral, we would walk every Sunday down Fifth Avenue and stop in the Plaza hotel to use the ladies room. Next to the immaculate sinks were bottles of Chanel No. 5 lotion and perfume.

I held on to Manny's Christmas boxes over the years, using them to store letters, postcards, and keepsakes. All my good memories are infused with the sweet scent of Givenchy fragrances. Their scent reminds me of how much little things meant to me after the important things—like how one smelled—faded away, lost their scent, their essence.

We always left for Atlantic City in pitch-black early morning darkness, like the other adrenaline junkies and addicts, and then crawled back onto a musty Greyhound bus with blue film over its windows in the dull saltwater scented afternoon. No matter how often we returned, New York City was always stark in contrast—clouds lined with thick exhaust, a crush of bodies everywhere, and our apartment bare, with equally empty refrigerator and cupboard.

Home was never really a respite for me—it was where the money ran out and we lived on charity, Mom's charm, and God's grace. Home was where I would watch Mom try to figure out what she was, what we were doing there, fumbling around in the dark. Mom was my first unreliable narrator—puzzle, arcade game to be solved…but she might never be. Just like the bleak Atlantic City arcades, life with Marguerite was a constant question of how to keep the game going long enough for me to figure it out and maybe master it.

I thought about games again the only time I remember Mom committing herself to a psychiatric hospital in Philadelphia in 2009. Just like living your life, games take risk and sometimes suspension of disbelief. I was also never any good at them. By then, I was living in Texas, where I had moved to keep a safe distance from her and our crazy past. She promised to visit, but she couldn't drive a car and, terrified of airplanes, she had never flown in her life.

It had taken more than a decade, but finally I got her to stop calling me multiple times a day, starting at five in the morning, ending sometimes close to midnight, sending me into a panic at all hours. The tone of her calls made it sound like she was living an emergency that only I could fix. The goal of the game between us was for me to rescue her. I learned halfway through that the way to win that game was to stop playing.

This began with her threatening my life as a teenager. I left a year later on scholarship to boarding school. Then I went to college in upstate New York. She followed me to Poughkeepsie when she was evicted from yet another apartment.

So after I graduated from college, I moved. I found that I couldn't really stay in one place. I chose work that meant that I was never still, never living somewhere long enough that Mom could pin me down. I stopped answering her every call, every e-mail right away. The only time the flurry of correspondence ever stopped was when she was in trouble.

This time, the man she was seeing loved heroin more than women, and it killed him. Mom tried going to Mass to talk to God about it, but she found herself overwhelmed by sadness. I'd heard it in her voice, in the once-a-week-on-Sunday-afternoon conversations I'd gotten her to agree to, when her voice was shaking and she sounded like she was sitting in the dark, whispering behind the sheets that doubled as curtains in her house. When a woman whose voice booms like thunder barely speaks loud enough for you to hear her, you know something is off. "Shan, I don't feel so good," she said to me. "But I'll be all right. Don't worry."

"What does that mean? Are you feeling OK? Do you need to go to the doctor?"

"No, nothing like that. I go to Jesus for all my needs. There's nothing a doctor can do for me."

"What about medication?" I asked delicately, with just a little hope in my voice.

"I don't want anything to interfere with my relationship with God."

I let it go. Once she started talking about God, there was no getting her to come back to me, to join me in the world of reason and logic. As much faith and devotion as I have in God, I also believe that God made therapy and medication to help his chemically imbalanced children.

But Mom knew the game. She had been to this dark place before. I knew because I had been with her.

For every reasonable, logical move my mother made, there was an unreasonable desire that led to moves that canceled out any reason at all. Instead of just coming to visit Manny in Atlantic City, Mom wanted to leave her Philadelphia house and the city where her benefits were established and were trying to lend some stability a life that was otherwise defined by chaos and life alone in the city.

My sister tried to honor my mother's requests, navigating options for moving our mother into assisted living in New Jersey, which, when she was successful, backfired.

Mom hated where she lived. She tried medication, and it made her feel different—I only spoke to her by phone during this time period, so I could hear the difference in how she sounded for myself. When she was hospitalized, her mania swayed her voice into non-comprehension, squeaky and soft, shaking. Talking to her shook me at my core, even thousands of miles away.

The woman would not, could not, live with other people for more than a few days without getting irritable and starting to complain. At the assisted living facility in New Jersey, she lasted less than a week.

Throughout the ordeals with her that my sister described, I felt guilty for being so removed from her life, but I also felt like distance was the healthiest, most necessary part of my self-preservation. I was not safe from what could only be described as her personal ambushes, even at boarding school when I spent the majority of three years in Troy, New York—a four-and-a-half-hour bus ride from New York City.

She did not surprise me often as a student as Emma Willard, but the second year I was there, she randomly responded to a mailed invitation to Parents' Weekend in the fall. It was during this visit that she casually informed me that she was in regular contact with Victor, whom I had never met and had just assumed was dead because she never said anything to me about him.

"He doesn't live that far from us," she said innocently. "He's just in Blackwood, outside of Philly. He wants you to write to him."

"Why can't he write to me? Why are you telling me this now?"

"Well, it just would be good for you to know your father, I guess. I don't know."

During my sophomore year at Vassar, Mom reminded me again that proximity to her would be more harmful than helpful to me in the long run. When she was finally evicted from our Bronx apartment—the last of several apartments we'd been evicted from in New York City—she moved a few blocks away from campus. She popped up on campus frequently enough that the cafeteria staff knew her name, that she worked at Stop and Shop a few miles away, and that she was my (proud) mother. She was so proud that, much to my chagrin, she carried my eighth grade graduation photo around with her to show everyone who I was.

No matter what I did, it felt like I could never truly be free of her. When I landed a Hearst Newspapers Journalism Fellowship that allowed me to move every six months for two years to a different mid-sized or large newspaper as a reporter, I was terrified and elated. I knew my fear and nightmares about everything that could go wrong were just signs that I needed to pursue something totally different in my life.

The fellowship began in Houston, where I worked for my first newspaper and learned how to drive on its six-lane highways. The best part of living there was that I was, for the first time, beyond my mother's spontaneous grasp, which was a blessing and a curse. On one hand, she wouldn't just pop up because she couldn't afford a plane ticket and didn't want to fly. On the other, cell phones were becoming increasingly popular even if cheap minutes were not.

In the Bronx and living in poverty with my mother, the phone became the center of my social life. It was entertaining to spend hours on the phone with my friends and boyfriends. It was a necessity to communicate with my restless mother and to be on constant alert that she might call with instructions or some idea of what she would be doing on any given day.

This ended up feeling familiar in my work as a journalist. The unpredictability and anxiety of my young life had prepared me for a professional life where it was never clear what might happen from one day to the next. Becoming a newspaper reporter introduced me to a different kind of dysfunctional family, one that accepted miscreants and do-gooders but mostly respected what you could produce and whether you could write or not more than what you looked like or where you were from.

So I dove in, letting myself be consumed with work. This is how I was when I lived in other cities: Beaumont, Seattle, San Francisco, Oakland, and Austin, which I thought would be my last stop. To paraphrase a statement that has been attributed to Lady Gaga, I knew I was never going to wake up one day and hear my career tell me it wasn't in love with me anymore. My writing and journalism careers kept me from coming unhinged. They each taught me how to live in a way that wasn't centered on fear of disaster.

So when my mother had a mental crisis that resulted in her committing herself to a psychiatric ward, I doubled down on work until I found that I couldn't anymore. Rita was in closest proximity to Mom then. While I felt guilty that she bore the brunt of caring for Mom, I also felt undone by the idea that I would have to do it again. After so many years away from her, I was unnerved by how little it took to feel uprooted by what was happening in Mom's life. I needed to feel grounded, safe.

━━┥┝━━

I've killed almost every houseplant I've ever owned, but in 2009, I wondered if prayer and belief in magic and Texas sun could help with outdoor plants. I bought a shovel and a few plants, and then I went to work putting them in the ground. I accumulated the true tools of a gardener: foam kneepads, a hand trowel, gloves, string, and old running sneakers. It was almost like I knew what I was doing. Mostly, it was therapy.

I tried to keep my flesh away from the ravenous, blistering fire ants in my growing crabgrass and weed wilderness by planting things at a distance, standing on my feet and bending over until my lower back ached. Of course, a main part of the game of life means that you cannot garden, like you cannot reckon with challenges, from a distance. I always had to get back down in the weeds, to pull insanity out from its roots.

And as hot as it was, there was something healing for my eight-year-old inner homeless girl in putting my hands in the earth, grounding my body and my spirit, remembering that I owned this land. The dirt on my hands and even my body aches planted me in the present. Putting plants in the ground let me grow something that wanted to live.

I hadn't worked the soil or amended the sandy loam dirt or pulled any of the weeds to give those plants a healthy start. When Mom had even a tiny patch of tomatoes in Brookhaven, they seemed to flourish in spite of her neglect, as I had. It was one of the features of her mania that made her seem magical.

My sweat, effort, and intention couldn't replicate the distant nurture she modeled, and it only made me more depressed. I did not accept my mother being ill and messing up my world with her mental problems. Parched, I paused in the garden, looking at the dark mounds of dirt.

Grubs—milky bugs with dull orange heads—reminded me of the small part of me that waited for and even wanted my mother to die. I had confessed it for the first time to a therapist in a hushed tone, refusing to explain my selfish motivations for saying such a thing because I was so ashamed of myself. "She will be better off dead," I said. "At least she would be free."

It was only partially what I meant. By the time I could say it aloud, I was grown, and I told myself I would be fine without a mother. Still, I held out hope that in the absence of me doing anything or saying anything, Marguerite would magically survive her darkest impulses and wake up one day and be the woman I had always dreamed she could be: whole and normal. Ready to show up for me.

But life kept showing me that my hope was misplaced. If she wasn't going to be a mother, it would have been simpler, less painful, and easier for her to just die like those plants did the day after I planted them. After her brief hospital stay, she stayed with Rita, her husband, and my niece and nephew while they figured out, again, what to do with her.

When Atlantic City didn't work out, Rita moved Mom in officially. But that arrangement was short-lived, because Mom was erratic and could still be abusive without warning. The rage and violence that was all too familiar resurfaced when Mom flew off the handle at one of the kids. Rita rightfully sent Mom back to her own devices, scrambling to get her Section 8 back so she could return to living on her own in Philadelphia.

We wanted her contained for her own safety, but she refused to be caged by anything or anyone. I secretly rooted for her freedom while I was frustrated by her inability to compromise, to make do with whatever life offered. Nothing was ever good enough or just right. Even when she was winning the game, she was never ahead.

CHAPTER 5
PRAY

SHUNDA RE: TWO MIRACLES OUR LORD HAVE GIFTED ME WITH

SHUN I NEED TO LET YOU KNOW ABOUT THE POWER OF PRAYER

I AM IN THE LIBRARY IN COLUMBIA SOUTH CAROLINA AND IT IS INDEED VERY WARM HERE ABOUT 72 DEGREES UNLIKE PHILADELPHIA WHERE IT WAS 40 DEGREES WITH SNOW WHEN I LEFT FOR COLUMBIA SOUTH CAROLINA ON WEDNESDAY.

I LOVE YOU AND MISS YOU SO VERY MUCH EVEN THOUGH I E-MAIL YOU AND SPEAK TO YOU ON THE TELEPHONE.

BUT HERE GOES THE TWO (2) MIRACLES.

I SPENT THE NIGHT AT HARRAH'S IN ATLANTIC CITY AND THEY WAITED TWO LATE TO TAKE THE MONIES FOR THE ROOM IT ACTUALLY WAS ONLY THE TAX BECAUSE THE ROOM WAS FREE BUT THE $11.00 STILL OVERDREW MY ACCOUNT BECAUSE I ONLY HAD $4.00 IN MY ACCOUNT TO KEEP IT OPEN UNTIL I GET MY CHECK.

THIS RACIST BANK RECEPTIONIST TOLD ME THAT I WAS OVERDRAWN $6.40 CENTS AND THE OVERDRAWN AMOUNT STARTING ON THAT DAY WOULD BE $33.00 PLUS THE OVERDRAWN AMOUNT WHICH BROUGHT IT UP TO $39.40. I TOLD HER THAT I DID NOT HAVE THAT AMOUNT AND ASKED HER IF WAITED FOR MY CHECK HOW MUCH WOULD THAT BE SHE SAID FOR TWO WEEKS THAT WOULD BE $78.00 OR MORE. AT THAT POINT I LOOKED AT HER AND SAID YOU KNOW WHAT I'LL BE BACK.

I WALKED OUT OF THE BANK AND WAS ENTERING THE FARMER'S MARKET ACROSS THE STREET AND LOOKED DOWN AND NOT TO KID YOU. I FOUND $41.00. SHUNDA I DO MEDITATE EACH MORNING AND I KNOW THAT WAS NOT A COINCIDENCE AND OUR LORD WAS WATCHING OVER ME.

THE OTHER MIRACLE WAS THAT I NEEDED TO PAY MY LIGHT BILL AND I ASKED MANNY TO LET ME HAVE SOME MONIES AND I WOULD REPAY HIM WHEN I GET MY MONIES APRIL 3RD AND HE COULDN'T DO IT BECAUSE OF HIS BILLS.

I VISITED HIM IN ATLANTIC CITY AND SPENT THE NIGHT AND BEFORE I GOT ON THE BUS I WENT TO BALLY AND PUT $20.00 IN THE MACHINE AND I GOT 2 DOUBLES PLUS 3 7'S @ 90 TIMES WHICH GAVE ME $218.00 AND I WAS ABLE TO PAY MY LIGHT BILL IN COLUMBIA SOUTH CAROLINA WITH THAT MONEY. I KNOW THAT GAMBLING IS NOT SPIRITUAL BUT THAT TIME MY PRAYERS WERE HEARD AND ONCE AGAIN I DID PRAY AND I MEDIATE EACH MORNING. SO PLEASE READ YOUR BIBLE AND REMEMBER PRAYERS WORK.

Watching my mother in motion meant seeing miracles as matter; it meant viewing the world through the eyes of a woman who believed herself to be a conduit for random acts of mercy and grace. Because she found God in slot machines and on sidewalks, by the time we were in church together, it felt to me as if she infused Jesus in church and not the other way around. To say there was something special about learning devotion and how to pray from a bipolar woman is an understatement.

Prayers were not just words she uttered to activate her connection to a far-flung universe but invocations that seemed to manifest serendipity from stubborn faith. Her belief in a God whose works and hands were mostly invisible to both of us was so strong that I knew it had been earned somehow, but I could not figure out exactly how it all worked. Our life together was so chaotic and unpredictable, it seemed realistic to at least try to appeal to God whether or not I understood what I was supposed to believe.

In church, I closed my eyes as she closed hers. I have no idea how much money she spent on my first communion for the brief time between fourth and fifth grade when she enrolled me in a Catholic School in midtown Manhattan, but none of it was cheap. Like any of her other purchases and decisions, I never questioned her choices. I just did what I was told.

Of all the things Mom passed on to me, faith was a major component to shaping my life and resilience. Learning to love God also helped me with a persistent, nagging loneliness. The hours between when school was out and Mom returned home in the evenings around ten o'clock were long. And it wasn't so much that she wasn't physically present as much as parents should be, it was more that even when she was around, we didn't really talk most of the time.

So my road to faith and belief began like the shape of the rest of my identity—with reading. I read the Bible, front to back, back to front, even the obscure and dry Old Testament, which I have never been able to retain. The New Testament has always been closer to my heart, in part because I can understand it just fine and also because all the narratives about Jesus that resonate with me are there.

My first prayers to God were asking him to help me understand what I was supposed to believe about Him. I also wondered about moral flexibility. I felt clean and whole and safe and protected when I read the Bible, just like I felt in church. Of course, I always ended up lost in other books: Harlequin romances, tawdry Jackie Collins novels, *The Color Purple* and Alice Walker's essays and poems, Sidney Sheldon, and, when I was feeling brave, Stephen King. I decided that if Mom could see God's hand even in gambling, I could find God in distant romantic scenes conjured by random writers. My prayers were to write like them, or to live like the families on television, my main babysitter and companion.

In between evictions, my steady diet of television taught me to believe that I was living a life that was not normal. I could feel it, the way you know that something doesn't fit you without checking to see how different its actual size is from yours, but because my world was limited to the universe of my mother's whims and consequences of her actions (or sometimes lack of action), it was hard to know.

On television, normal children—even the ones who were poor—had both mothers and fathers. More than that, they had at least one parent who was not erratic, secretive, and crazy. They seemed to know how to stay put in one place with a community of familiar faces, but we were constantly on the move.

In one sense, it was exciting to never know what was coming next. But it was also terrifying not to be a part of a community, or even know how to be a part of one.

It was confusing trying to reconcile the world Mom and I lived in with the glorious heaven she always talked about. In real life, case workers and other local and state bureaucrats shoved paperwork and lingo at her, deadlines and rules she disregarded like it was her mission in life to get over, though truly she seemed to be uninterested in following any rules that weren't divine from the outset. If we served a mighty God, why did he let us run out of money to pay rent and buy groceries? Where was God when we joined the faithful and unfaithful alike at Salvation Army soup kitchens on holiday nights? Jesus loved the poor and the meek, and we were both—but why did God's love require such constant desperation?

In the biblical narratives Mom liked to watch, it was the disobedient children of God who incurred his wrath, while the faithful were saved from drowning in the Red Sea or sacrificing their children or even giving up their own lives. In exchange for worship and unquestioning belief (the latter is where I struggled most) God delivered them peace, places to live, food to eat. I was comforted by this notion, even though it seemed to have some logical flaws. That was a long time ago and far away. All those people were white, and a lot of them were men.

Still, watching my mother surrender to God helped shape my own relationship to faith and hope. If nothing else, our weekly journey to Mass in Manhattan offered us a routine—one thing I could be sure of when I could be sure of little else.

＞＜＋＋＞＜

Our Sundays began with me stumbling to my bedroom window and noticing dew frosting the windows of cars parked in a line connected like sausage links along the sidewalks. Mom would spin around the apartment, checking the gas at the stove for no good reason, so that I heard the *click whoosh* of the stove pilot light while I was washing up and getting dressed. From the bathroom, I heard rushing in a short burst from the kitchen faucet and remembered that there were times in Chester when running water wasn't a given.

Hugging a too-small towel, I rummaged through my small pile of clothes for one of my wrinkled dresses in a torn-up box, the closest to the closet door in a crevice filled with boxes bulging with old paper and roaches. The radiator clinked like a man inside was beating at the metal with a stick, a tiny spout on the side sputtering and spitting water or steam.

At the corner of my stack of mattresses, the sun streamed directly onto my skinny legs, warming my ankles and feet as I smoothed greasy Vaseline over my knees and elbows and pulled on shoes. Our outfits were both for Jesus and for our ritual long Manhattan walk to the Metropolitan Museum of Art and Central Park.

Between fourth and fifth grade was the last year Mom received her miracle money— the lawsuit settlement checks. She had moved us to a tiny furnished studio apartment in midtown Manhattan. We lived there for several months, within walking distance of Saint Patrick's Cathedral, before we were evicted and sent to a family shelter and then back to the same section of the Bronx in a different low-income apartment building on a street blocks over from where we had lived years before.

From the Bronx, we took two or three trains and had to leave our apartment by eight thirty to make it to ten fifteen Mass downtown. Walking in, every time, was like a prayer of its own. The heavy brass doors at the entrance were so tall it felt like walking into heaven. We paused at the immaculate grayish-white marble pillars holding holy water, the residue of so many worldly hands that had dipped into it to make the sign of the cross at their foreheads and chests collecting at the bottom of the water in gray clouds. Frankincense filled my nose, and pews reflected soft light streaming in through stained glass. The church was usually filled with people by the time Mom and I shuffled in, except for the pews on the sides or in the back. Mom always liked to be in the first row, like she would get extra credit from God for sitting way up front, but she would settle for the second or third pew as long as we were close to the aisle. That way we could be among the first to get communion. Marguerite's church strategy left me in awe, and that was before we even sat down.

A friend of mine who is a United Methodist Church pastor once said an African bishop told him that at white churches, congregants worship from the neck up, but black people worship with their whole bodies. My Mom was the perfect example of what he meant.

We were typically the only two black women in the Catholic parishes we frequented, so the difference between her shouting the lyrics of Catholic hymns and the low murmur of other voices around us was always evident. She didn't just say her prayers from memory like the others around us, she performed them with her whole face, spitting them out. I cringed every time.

Aside from Mom's other Southern qualities, like her affection for fried whiting fish, Carolina white rice, and okra, it was the shouting that reminded me that my mother was country. "Mom!" I would start most of my sentences to her, in church or outside. "You're *yelling*."

"I'm not yelling, Shan. That's just how I talk," she would say in a strained, loud whisper.

If her inside voice sounded like she was talking to you as if you were across the street instead of sitting right next to her, imagine her singing in her outside voice: a blaring, nasal, off-key tone.

It might not have been so bad if people didn't stare with their mouths agape at the echo of her booming, broken falsetto through the church; but then, people were always staring at us. My frequent little girl prayer during her ruckus was to learn to deal with the stares without hanging my head in shame. I was almost always unsuccessful.

In the quiet moments of Mass, I began to see the differences between Mom and me. I preferred the soft, deferential Hail Marys I could hear as the delicate beads of her blue rosary passed through her heavy fingers during Novenas in the smaller chapel at the back of Saint Patrick's on Saturdays. The silence offered me comfort and a window into her nature when she was still. I could feel the magic of a bigger, divine presence when it was quiet, like everything that had happened to us was laid bare and wiped clean. The knot of anxiety and fear lodged in my chest started to loosen up. I did not feel as lonely or isolated or forgotten by angels.

Another of my many prayers to God and his saints was that Mom and I would find a peaceful place to sleep, a steady way to be in the world. I didn't understand how God could be so far and so close at the same time, but even with my unresolved questions, I figured it couldn't hurt to send up prayers. I wondered in those moments about my mother's past, about how she had become so devoted to an invisible father when she had only briefly mentioned her biological one.

She said his name once or twice my whole life, and our distant relatives said that her grandfather had been an academic. Learning that I was planning to write this book, Johnnie Ann became more guarded with details, though she never said why. I had only been to Orangeburg, South Carolina, as an infant, so I had no memory of it.

Maybe Mom's life there was so bad that it had sparked her rebellion from the heart of Southern Black life, leading her to convert to Catholicism at eighteen. Maybe it was a simple choice to find a faith that offered her God in a way that she could better understand. He was, as far back as I could remember, at the center of the dreams and visions she tracked by scrawling on the bright white walls of our apartment in ballpoint pen.

That Jesus had been a kind of orphan, born in the winter like me, endeared me to him. The spirit of Jesus led me when I would read the Bible and again when I would grow up to have no fewer than five versions of scripture in my home. He was a maverick, led by his faith and commitment, despite all the people who stared at him and doubted the power of his faith in humanity. He was a defender of the poor, of people like my mom and me, so I grew up loving that Jesus, even if I wasn't a big fan of his followers. I felt like I knew him intimately, too, through my mother's year-round fixation on movies like *The Ten Commandments*, which I watched enough to memorize most of the lines, and *Jesus of Nazareth*.

Marguerite mentioned God so often that I cannot remember a conversation in which religion didn't come up, though I always sensed that her definition of a miracle would be disputed by anyone else. I liked that she found God in Lotto tickets or in what most people would simply call coincidence. If God had made everything, he'd made Marguerite, faithful sinner that she was.

The way she connected miracles to money, too, made me think of finance as the result of prayer more than work. Over the years, she would leave me voicemails and send letters and e-mails, proclaiming a miracle that was usually connected to money. We would be walking down a crowded New York street, and something would tell me to look down, and there would be a folded twenty-dollar bill underfoot.

"It's a miracle, Shan; Lord have mercy," Mom would say. "Thank you, Jesus."

For someone who spent so much time in church, I responded to proclamations of miracles very differently. I asked God to forgive me as I used the long wooden sticks planted in sand below rows of candles to dig dollar bills out of the donation slots. I knew stealing was wrong, but I didn't always have the patience to wait for a selective miracle from an inconsistent angel.

The harder our lives got, the hungrier we were, the more Mom wanted to go to Mass. I wondered if prayer fed her resourcefulness or if it was the other way around. Just as she could find churches giving out canned peaches and pork and pasta, she could find a Catholic church no matter where we were living.

To become the paralegal God wanted her to be, for instance, she took night classes at Career Blazers in Manhattan and at Bronx Community College. Where Italian and theater classes fit into her dreams wasn't entirely clear, but she liked the professor. She couldn't afford to pay someone to watch me, so I sat next to her as a second and third grader. She'd rip out a few pages from her notebook and hand me a pen, trying to whisper, "I think the professor has a crush on me."

I would look over at her and nod slowly. The professor, a balding guy with a bushy mustache, never made eye contact with either of us. Because Marguerite lived outside of the realm of possibility, though, it never struck me as impossible that her hunches were anything but true.

She was also superstitious. On our way home a few blocks from the school, Mom bent down, knees together like a swinging door to one side of her body in a dainty closed-leg squat to pick up stray pennies on the street. She believed you should not walk past money in the street or under ladders, or any construction site paraphernalia. Whenever I walked on the far end of a pole on the street separating us, she would double back and walk on my side, muttering, "Shan, don't split the pole. Jesus."

If Mom ever noticed that people were perplexed by her presence, she never let on. I frowned at the adults who stared, defensive and annoyed that they would go out of their way to make us feel unwelcome. Saks Fifth Avenue was her favorite place to window shop and try on dresses we would never even dare to try and steal.

Mom collected perfume samples, stuffing them in her purse one after another as snooty saleswomen raised their eyebrows at her and the paper bulged from inside. We were probably the poorest regulars they saw in the store, given my mother's complete disregard for any of their judgment. After an hour or so of touring the different floors—children's, evening gowns, business wear—she would take my hand and led me out of the store.

If she had a few dollars, Mom would buy me a coveted Dove ice cream bar or a hot sausage with boiled onions and mustard. I devoured whatever small meal she could afford by the time we got to the giant toy store, F.A.O. Schwarz, where I ran free for an hour and would pocket small Hello Kitty pens before we walked through Central Park.

Because she was an orphan, too, I think this simple routine of ours was part of my mother's natural instinct. It brought me joy to have these moments of relief from a life that was otherwise dark and without cheer. This joy was its own kind of prayer. Exposure to a world that most people's dreams were made of gave me a blueprint for the kind of future I wanted for myself—it added to the idea that there was a universe of prayers answered and dreams fulfilled in the world.

There was a stark difference between that ritzy world we visited and reality. After one Sunday full of outings, I saw the clear gap between our reality and the dream life we wandered through in Manhattan. After an hour-long train ride back to the Bronx, I remembered that we were between checks, and it would be at least a week before we could afford groceries or rent. As we walked back to the apartment, I noticed a row of six black garbage bags, sagging like full bellies on the curb. Peeking through one of the bags was my favorite sweater, bubblegum pink with a white rabbit sporting green sunglasses on the front. We had been evicted again.

"Jesus, Mary, and Joseph," Mom said, pausing to look at our discarded belongings. We turned on our heels to walk away from our clothes and keepsakes, including the only picture of Jose that my mother still owned.

⊰⊱

OUR HEAVENLY FATHER IS THERE FOR ALL OF US AND HE PUTS OUR GUARDIAN ANGELS IN CHARGE OF ALL OF US.

WE HAVE TO KEY IN TO OUR LORD AND HIS WISHES AND HIS COMMANDS BECAUSE HE IS ALWAYS LOOKING OUT FOR OUR BEST INTERESTS. HE GRANTS WHAT WE WANT ONLY IF IT IS NOT HARMFUL TO US. REMEMBER THAT SHUNDA BECAUSE THAT IS SO IMPORTANT.

I AM PROUD OF YOU AND PROUD THAT OUR LORD HAS BLESSED YOU WITH SO MUCH FAITH, HOPE AND STRENGTH, NOW I BELIEVE THE MESSAGE IS THAT HE TOLD YOUR GUARDIAN ANGEL AND MINE IS THAT HE WANTS YOU TO CONTACT HIM, I KNOW THAT SOUNDS SILLY BECAUSE AS YOU SAY AND I BELIEVE YOU THAT YOU TALK TO GOD AND READ HIS BIBLE, BUT MAYBE, JUST MAYBE THERE'S SOMETHING MISSING, JUST TRY THIS PRAYER AND LET ME KNOW WHAT HAPPENS WHEN I E-MAIL YOU NEXT WEEK HERE GOES.

OUR FATHER, WHICH ARE IN HEAVEN, HOLLOW BE THINE NAME, THOU KINGDOM COME THINE WILL BE DONE ON EARTH AS IT IS IN HEAVEN. GIVE US THIS DAY OUR DAILY BREAD AND FORGIVE US OUR TRESPASSES AS WE FORGIVE THOSE WHO TRESPASS AGAINST US AND LEAD US NOT INTO TEMPTATION BUT DELIVER US FROM EVIL FOR THINE IS THE POWER AND GLORY FOREVER AND FOREVER AMEN.

REMEMBER YOU ARE VERY SPECIAL (GOD BLESS YOU)

AND AS USUAL, I LOVE YOU WITH ETERNAL LOVE, YOUR MOM

CHAPTER 6
CHOOSE YOUR BATTLES WISELY

When the money from Jose's death ran out, we were entirely dependent on prayer, welfare, and handouts to survive. Of course, it was not the kind of thing that my mother would have explained to me. I only guessed at the change because of the increased frequency with which Marguerite and I spun through the Bronx, our days spent sitting, waiting, and begging—in the check-cashing place, at the welfare office, in the soup kitchen line, at the church pantry, at the Emergency Assistance Unit.

Part of how I came to love education and books was that my only real breaks from visits to social service agencies and churches were school and the library. By the time I was in fifth grade, I had attended six different schools, most of them public. The last public school was C.S. 67, a cavernous four-story building several blocks from the Bronx Zoo, with grated gates alongside the stairs as if students might toss themselves over the side into the lobby at any moment.

The stairs were as quiet at the end of the school day as the main reading room of the West Farms branch of the New York Public

Library, the light as soft as the single forty-watt bulb above the bedroom Mom let me have while she slept on the old couch in our living room. To stay grounded, I pored through homework with the same quiet focus I felt in church. I would tackle each assignment one problem at a time, like all the other parts of our lives.

Months before I would graduate as valedictorian from the lowest-track of sixth grade, Ms. Boswell asked me to stay after class when all the other students had gone. She was a tall, pear-shaped woman—one of a special few teachers from my childhood that remains crystal clear in my memory. She wore her hair in a permed mushroom, and she had big plump cheeks that she dusted with bright pink blush.

Ms. Boswell slipped me an application to a private school for poor, gifted minority students in Manhattan called De La Salle Academy with the same discretion she used when she left small shopping bags of used clothes for me in the coat closet. She said something gentle but firm like, "You should think about going here." She implied that there was no question I would get in.

She told me to get my mother to fill it out, which I knew meant that I would have to fill it out myself, just as I had applied for my mother's Section 8 housing as a fourth grader. Multiple evictions had taught me that paperwork was not one of Mom's gifts.

Students had to test into De La Salle Academy, which was then located on the top floor of Holy Name School on West Ninety-seventh Street. There were just a couple hundred students in three grades. De La Salle was founded by Christian Brothers and spearheaded by an Irish bear of a man named Brother Brian Carty. Mom was convinced she was in the presence of a saint the moment she met him.

Brother Brian certainly looked the part in his all-black clerical clothing, towering over us, usually without his white collar, which he only wore on special occasions. Most mornings, he was perched on a little stool, his long legs extended out like he was comfortable there, though he couldn't have been, the sound of classical music soaring above a stream of children lined up to greet him before he rang the brass bell signaling the start of classes for the day.

Girls like me got morning hugs, his hazel brown eyes smiling to match the curved line of his mouth beneath a thicket of mustache. As he pumped the hands of my male classmates vigorously, he also fixed his eyes on their collars, checking for ties. Dress code was business casual, and if they weren't wearing neckties, he sent them to a large drawer that held a collection of old tacky ones with wild prints.

De La Salle was an hour-long train ride from East Tremont, where we'd found a subsidized apartment after a short stay at a couple of shelters in Queens. Mom accompanied me to school for the first few weeks, just to make sure it was OK. She also liked that the school had a neighbor in Holy Name Catholic Church.

She always gave me a parting kiss on the forehead, and then disappeared into the dimly lit church while I climbed five flights of stairs like I was going to the mountaintop. Not long after I started there, we were evicted from our apartment on Tiebout Avenue too. Before long, I went to school smelling like the Brooklyn shelter where we stayed: no-frills soap, sweat, and piss.

If Brother Brian ever noticed that I smelled bad, he never said a word. I was a loner anyway, so it wasn't hard to stay away from the other students in our small classes so they wouldn't catch a whiff of me. I concentrated on language arts, history, biology, and Spanish.

I loved our social justice class the most because we got to volunteer to visit the elderly or bring them food with Meals on Wheels. It felt good to know that other people were having a hard time and that even though I was going through similar poverty and depression, I could do something to help someone else.

The combination of Brother Brian's gentle and generous demeanor, the academically challenging classes, and the smaller school all helped to make me feel, finally, like I belonged to something other than just Marguerite. Then there was talk therapy. A wild-haired older white guy named Mike Harris ran the first therapy group I joined. Some of my classmates needed a little extra help, another ear, like me. Until Mike Harris, I had kept my thoughts to myself or written them in the notebook that doubled as a journal.

With Mike Harris, we weren't allowed to stay quiet though. He wanted us to do exercises with partners, which was how I met my first real friend, Dana. She was a Bronx girl too, and everybody loved her because she was funny, pretty, and smart. She loved purple, which was evident in most of what she wore, and even though she was just a bit taller than five feet, she was loud enough that you never forgot she was around.

The rest of us hesitated to talk about what hurt us; Dana spoke up and said her piece. Her mother had raised her, her twin brother, and their two older siblings—who all would go on to attend Ivy League colleges—on her own. They lived in what had to have been the most luxurious and sweet-smelling apartment in Webster Projects.

Dana, and eventually her family, made me want to be braver than I thought I could ever be. I wanted to be like her, too—cute, petite, from an intact family. Still, when we first met and she asked for my phone number, I didn't tell her that I didn't have a phone because I was living in a shelter.

I hadn't ever said the world aloud, even. It was hard to talk about, and we were homeless so frequently that it seemed inevitable, like there was nothing anyone could do to keep it from happening to us. We slept on cots in large, dark rooms like the ones at the Roberto Clemente family shelter eight years before, this time a few shopping bags with our clothes and the papers Mom needed close by stuffed under our bodies so no one could take them without waking us.

So when Dana asked for my phone number, I gave her a fake one. I knew it was a mistake. The following Monday, she stepped in front of me after Brother Brian rang the bell, her jaw tight and her eyes steady but like tiny black half moons behind those thick glasses.

"That number you gave me didn't work."

"I know."

"Why did you give me a fake number?"

"Because I don't have a phone."

"Why didn't you tell me that?"

"Because," I said, my breath getting short. "I don't have a place to live."

We looked at each other. Around us, our classmates were deserting the hallway for homeroom. When it was just the two of us in the hallway between the blue lockers, she asked, "Does Brother Brian know that?"

"No, and I'm not telling him."

"You should tell him, Shunda," she said. She was fumbling with her backpack. "He should know what's going on. Maybe he can help you."

I had liked her so much in Mike Harris, our eponymous group therapy, even though the boy I liked was only into being her boyfriend. Now I felt like she was just interfering. "Let's work on the exercise after lunch, OK?"

She nodded and I thought that was the end of it. At De La Salle, no one knew that I had ever been separated from my mother once, and until Dana confronted me about the fake number, I hadn't thought about the combination of panic and relief I felt at the idea that I might be separated from Mom again. When I was five, I turned out OK without talking to anybody about our life. I thought I could do it again at thirteen. This was just a school like any other school, and teachers and principals would only do so much.

Before lunch, Brother Brian called me to his office. It was more like a cubbyhole layered with thank-you notes, programs, schedules, lists, grades, and articles. Behind him, on a filing cabinet, was a small, sleek black stereo system that was smaller than the one in the main hallway. He sat on a small chair and leaned back and forth in it like it was a rocking chair.

"Dana told you," I said.

"Yes, she told me. But I wish *you* would have told me. I'm going to make some calls and see what I can do to help," he said. "How long have you been homeless?"

It was a tricky question. We'd been at that shelter for a few weeks, but in truth we'd been homeless for as long as we'd lived in New York, with a few years and months of grace...of housing. In the days that followed, he talked to Mom a little more and got us settled in a welfare hotel on 103rd Street between Columbia University and De La Salle. Marguerite reacted to the news in his office by throwing her arms around him and clasping her hands over her open mouth. "Praise God, Brother Brian. Thank you. God bless you," she said. He nodded slowly and gave her the same sweet smile he gave everyone who came into De La Salle.

Months later, we moved back to the same section of the Bronx, near 183rd and Daly Avenue, still a few blocks from the Bronx Zoo, just closer to the train station. It was the last apartment I would share with Marguerite, though neither of us knew that when we first moved in. In that fifth-floor apartment, I would wait until Mom and most of the rest of the borough had gone to sleep, open a creaky metal gate to the fire escape, and sit outside under the sky. I would listen and watch the trains moving toward Manhattan or up to Pelham Parkway under moonlight and look for the brightest star in the sky. It was usually the only one.

━┼┝━

De La Salle was the first place I had ever been where people planned for the future like it was a given that we would go on to do great things. We were fighting for the best version of our future.

My experience in New York and Philly up until that point made me dubious; and I certainly didn't see how I could be great if I had to take care of myself and look out for my crazy mother.

Brother Brian encouraged us to think not just about high schools in the city but about boarding school. The idea of going to school somewhere else and getting away from Mom thrilled me, but it was also terrifying. The brochures depicted sanctuaries of manicured lawns, beautiful old buildings, and expansive laboratories and libraries. I told Dana about boarding school, and she looked at me like I was crazy, but she always did that.

On a group trip to New England schools, Mom joined me and a few other students and their parents on a weekend trip. One of my classmates' dads drove us in a rented minivan to see the schools in Massachusetts and Connecticut on a Saturday.

They were campuses of mini-mansions where Mom and I were instantly out of place. I wore a ten-dollar dress and Mom was in her standard fare, her purse bulging with old mail and that rosary of hers. The dream of leaving the city and going to one of these schools seemed further and further from ever becoming reality the longer we were on the road. We finally stopped to eat at a diner, and Mom and I ordered a simple lunch like everyone else.

Then the bill came.

"You have to pay for your lunch," my classmate's dad said.

"We don't have any money," my mother replied.

His eyebrows shot up into a dangerous-looking wrinkle and his eyes got wide. "Excuse me?"

"We don't have any money. I—I would have..." My mother always started to stutter when she was put on the spot. Shame erased her words. It was painful to listen to and I felt powerless to help her. It felt like my fault, somehow. I should have known she didn't have any money. She definitely couldn't pay for any of the schools we were visiting. She couldn't even pay for lunch.

"I can pay you back when we get to the city," I offered.

"You're a kid," he shot back. He turned his wide eyes back on her. "You're an adult. You should know better than to come on a trip without any money."

"I—I—know," Mom said. "I'm sorry."

"Well, sorry doesn't pay anybody's bills, does it?" He said this while digging into his wallet and fumbling angrily with cash. "Who goes on a trip without any money?" It was a point that obviously neither my mother nor I had considered.

He paid the bill, fuming the whole time, shaking his head. No one else said anything. When it was time for us to leave, Mom and I slunk into the van behind the rest of the small group, silent for the long, tense drive back to De La Salle. I watched the road, wondering what it would take for me to ever be like other kids, for us to be like other families, who at least had enough money for lunch and sometimes enough for fancy schools in faraway places.

⊱━━⊰

Most of my family gathered for the first time in my life at Holy Name Church for my De La Salle graduation. Rita, who was living abroad at the time as a missionary in the Middle East, brought her husband, Alphonso, and my niece Rachel with her from Egypt. She helped me buy a graduation dress: peach-colored with lace sleeves and big beige buttons. Dana wore purple; we dressed at her house on Webster Avenue before taking the train to De La Salle with our blue caps and gowns.

Ironically, she was going off to boarding school in Pennsylvania. I would not be so lucky. I didn't get financial aid to attend the school in Massachusetts that had admitted me, so Brother Brian arranged for me to go to a Catholic high school in the Bronx. In the meantime, I kept looking for a school that might be able to give me a scholarship.

After the whirlwind of graduation, I drew out my goodbye to Dana, whom I wanted to follow to Pennsylvania. Our borough, our city, was all we had known as friends. I was worried she would make new friends and forget about me, even though she kept saying she wouldn't.

I had found safety in her apartment, walking twenty blocks there and back, even at night. If Marguerite could wander the streets at all hours, I figured I could too. I was my mother's child. I had tried to be so different from her, but feeling stuck in the Bronx made me more rebellious.

Away from the watchful eye of Brother Brian and my friends at De La Salle, knowing that Dana would be off at school, I became a different kind of girl. I stopped caring about my future or any future. I started drinking and smoking weed when I was fourteen. If holding on tight to my dreams didn't make them any closer to reality, I wanted to see what it felt like to let them go. It would not be the last time I stopped fighting to be good. I met boys and let them do to me what they wanted, telling myself that even if these decisions would eventually make me feel ashamed and more worthless, what really mattered was that they were somehow comforting, maybe even empowering.

That this kind of recklessness hadn't landed my mother any long-term relationships was not lost on me, and my self-loathing deepened every time I lay down with someone and pretended that sex could create meaningful love. My mother's sporadic abuse made it easier for me to try and find ways to escape my feelings.

As pleasant as Marguerite was in public and at church with strangers, in the privacy of the apartments we shared, her darker side took over and her patience was thin. There were no usual days for us, but typically, she barely talked if she wasn't about to descend into a depression that made her seem like another woman altogether.

Imagine taking a walk home in the summer without an umbrella, scanning the bright blue sky for clouds and relaxing when you notice there's no reason to worry. Then, as soon as you look down, a sudden storm drenches you despite the fact that there had been no sign of rain for weeks. I felt that kind of sinking shock and surprise when Mom abused me, with her hands or with her words or both; it felt like dark clouds stuffed themselves into our small rooms and suffocated me with the thick humidity of confusing hatred.

Rita had seen this up close before she had fled. My family knew that Mom was capable of this kind of rage, but they felt helpless to combat it or figure it out, which left me as the only witness when I was growing up with her. Marguerite would pace like a caged bull, her feet padding in quick succession up and down a hallway while she muttered or screamed.

I have to get out of here. There are drug dealers everywhere. It's not safe. My God, it's not safe. And this child. I don't know what to do with this child. God help me. I wish I never had her. I wish she'd never been born.

She lunged at me to grab me violently from my sleep, waking me up if I was in bed with punches near my ribs or shoulders, until I woke up, without fighting, untangling myself from the covers. I figured if I just let her do whatever she wanted, the one-sided fight would be shorter. It was torturous and painful, the kind of thing that made me hate myself the way she seemed to hate me. Only a bastard child could deserve to be hit like that, and she hadn't really wanted me anyway. In my worst moments, I believed I was just alive because Jose hadn't lived.

I never tried to fight her because I knew she wasn't herself and she was my mother. *Children are not supposed to hit their mothers*, I would recite to myself. Still, I knew that one day I would have to fight her back; I just had to decide when. These episodes of hers, when she seemed possessed by something that was so unclear to me, lasted minutes, usually never longer than an hour, though I lost track of time. I don't remember what I thought about or how I felt, but I know that I would hold my breath and let the tears come. I couldn't wipe them away because she would have my hands pinned. If I tried to say anything she would scream louder, spit sprinkling my face from the force of her words.

The first few times she hit me, I figured that maybe if she heard my voice, she would remember that I loved her. Maybe it was like those Disney movies where a monster could be transformed by a kiss or a witch could be returned to her former glory with the right combination of words. But when she was spinning out of control like that, the sound of my voice seemed to make her more agitated, and it made the punches feel even harder.

With the heaviness of her on my body, I prayed for her to die. I hated myself for what seemed like such an unnatural impulse, but I wanted her to be gone, and I didn't want to be the one to kill her. I knew that the woman who claimed to love me more than life also lived in the same body that would eventually threaten to kill me, which was the only thing that kept me from really hating her completely.

When she wasn't manic, she did try to show me she loved me by writing me love notes most mornings before leaving for hours. These small gestures made her sporadic bullying worse, because I couldn't understand how someone who professed such constant, abiding love could punch me with the force usually reserved for a hostile stranger.

One night before summer ended, I was on the phone after midnight in my room. It had been months since my mother had had one of her episodes, since she had tried to beat me. There was no indication, no warning that she would try again that night, until she yelled from the living room: "Who are you in there talking to?"

"Nobody, Ma," I said back. Whomever it was, I said a hasty good night and hung up the plastic red phone. Moments after, Mom was at the door, her footfall heavy, the sound of a basketball bouncing through a tiny corridor.

"Get up! Get out of bed." She was breathing heavy, each word a yank at my clothes and my body, rough on my flesh. It had been so long since she had attacked me that I had forgotten how to escape it in my head. She wasn't making any sense, her face moist with beads of sweat. Her mouth was saying, *I hate you, you demon, I hate you. I wish I never had you. You hear me?* Her hot flesh closed around my thin frame, her legs over mine, her arms pinning mine to the bed, spittle from the gap in her front teeth spraying my cheeks. *I hate you. I'll kill you. I'll kill you.*

Her hands were on my throat now, her eyes the same as ever: beautiful, deep brown, her frayed wig obscuring the lightbulb above our heads, like a cop interrogating a suspect. My mother was in there, I thought as her punches landed on my arms, along my rib cage. I deserved it, I thought. I deserved to die because I was a burden and I was fresh and maybe her life would have been easier without me. I prayed for her to make good on her promise.

I might have called her mommy, pleaded with her to stop hurting me, please. The punches eased, like the last raindrops of a passing storm. She leaned back, on her feet, off the bed, looking at me like she had just awakened from a spell. Her hands slipped down to her sides and she said, "Oh, God." I turned on my side, watching her, tears on my face.

I curled up and buried my face in the pillow. How could she talk about God now? Where was he in this?

She slinked away, back to the bed she'd made for herself on the couch, and wailed. I woke up to her apology. She said sorry, kissed me on my forehead, and left me a two-page letter. I pretended to be asleep until I heard the click of her heels disappear out of our building, then I darted into the kitchen, grabbed a fresh trash bag, tossed my clothes, a few old books, and shoes in it, and carried them to Dana's apartment.

That's your mother, everyone said. *You can't just leave her.*

I don't want to die, I repeated. But most of them had only ever seen her benevolence. They could not imagine her abuse or how it tormented me. I said the same thing to Dana, to the police who showed up at her apartment, to Brother Brian, to the social workers who eventually got us in a room together a week later.

I didn't want to go to foster care again either. I was four years from being old enough to be on my own. There was still hope for boarding school. I could still get out, Brother Brian told me. I just had to hang on.

When I carried my trash bag of things back to Daly Avenue, I barely said a word to my mother. It took her almost a year before she tried to hit me again. I caught her fist when she cornered me near a window, and I said, "You will not hit me again, or I will hit you back."

She stuttered this time. She gave me the same wide-eyed look as before. "Are you crazy?" she finally said.

"I don't want to fight you," I said. "You're my mother."

I let her fist go. She looked in my face, and for the first time, I saw a glimpse of her as a little girl. Before, I had only been able to see my own helplessness, not hers. She walked away crying. Instead of feeling victorious for winning a battle over my most intimate bully, I was devastated and sad.

⋟╫╪⋞

I started to fall apart. It was not the obvious way my mom fell apart, which was like a house filled with porcelain and china caving in and sending everything breaking and flying in a loud crash of total destruction. I fell apart slowly, internally at first, knowing without caring that this could have external repercussions or consequences.

But I was fundamentally aware that no one, not even my mother, was really paying much attention to me. I was a teenager, but

I was flat-chested and awkward. I talked too proper from reading too many books, even though I could compare notes on street cred with the best of my neighbors and classmates.

Even among the outsiders, I was an outsider—both a nerd and an introvert before they were trendy. If Mom noticed that I was starting to act out, she didn't say. She only warned me when we were watching Geraldo Rivera once that I could get pregnant if I was having sex. "God wants you to wait," she would say.

I believed that God wanted me to have something of my own, some joy and comfort of my own creation. But mostly, I gave up caring about what God wanted. I was trying to figure out what *I* wanted, and I believed that if I fought for whatever it was, I might just be able to get it.

As a freshman at Aquinas High School, I ran track for a full semester until I got bored. I broke a record in the 1600 meters, but then, instead of chasing more records, I began to chase boys. I had studied Marguerite's ways for years, so I thought I could try on her addiction to men without any trouble.

Using money from my summer jobs, I bought myself a few new pairs of jeans and fake hair that I taught myself to weave into long box braids. I wasn't as fly as a lot of the girls in the Bronx, but I thought I was pretty cute. So did James, my high school sweetheart. The first time he showed up at our Bronx apartment doorstep to take me out, my mother took one look at him and her smile faded.

James was a big, burly, menacing-looking guy with a fake front tooth he could click in and out of place. He'd lost the original in a fight. To me, he looked like a bodyguard, but everyone else said he looked like trouble. He had a part-time job working at the Columbus Boys and Girls Club, not far from where he was supposed to be going to class at Dewitt Clinton High School. The rest of the time, he sold weed. We met through a friend of mine at Aquinas.

We were inseparable. He was about 250 pounds, six feet to my five foot ten, just over 100-pound frame. His little brother, Duck, followed him like a shadow and could barely contain his crush on me.

Their mother was an imposing nurse. Her hair was always done in a French roll that came together in a tight, long, slick bun that hovered above the back of her neck and was decorated with golden stars and balls stuck in with wide bobby pins.

"A Catholic school girl, huh?" she said the first time I met her. I had been fooling around with James after school in the apartment. Duck was outside playing in the street, always within James's earshot. The bedroom they shared was much darker than my own on Daly Avenue and filled with piles of boy stuff everywhere: a dresser, a TV, a Nintendo console, and musty clothes tossed every which way on the floor.

I loved him hard and deep because he knew the kind of poverty that I lived in; he lived in it too. When I was with him, I felt strong and invincible, like money didn't matter at all. Heart was the thing. We were Bronx-hearted—staying out late, drinking forties, smoking weed. He carried me up five flights of stairs at least once when I stayed out until two in the morning with him and his uncle, pissy drunk and high when Mom answered the door without a word and let it slam behind me. Maybe she knew the time would come for us to talk about it; it just wasn't right then.

≖⊰╫⊱≖

I managed to apply to boarding school and get pregnant within months of each other, at least this is what I remember about the beginning of 1993. Because nothing in my experience had prepared me for the possibility of getting what I wanted, which I decided was to live far away from Marguerite and start fresh, to become my own woman, I stopped keeping track of possibilities and started to sink into the realities of life in the Bronx.

By the second semester of my freshman year in high school, several of my classmates were pregnant and dropping out. I had gotten into a silly fight with a bully who threatened to fight me after school for stepping on her new shoes, even though I wasn't standing anywhere close to her. When I came to school with a straight-edge razor tucked into my cheek (James' idea), a nun discovered it when the bully and I got into a shouting match in the hallway the day we were supposed to fight. I was suspended for the first and only time in my life.

I still loved school, but I blew off class except for social studies and English. I started thinking that the girls who were about to become teenage moms were on to something. Maybe my safety net could be having a baby with James, even if doing so wouldn't come without a fight.

Everything was already a battle anyway. James brought groceries to the apartment one evening, and Mom snapped at him. "We don't need you," she sneered, after he put the bags on the counter near the aluminum double sink we never used. "We don't need your charity."

"I never said you did, Miss Marguerite," he said back, uncommonly calm. He never called anybody by Miss Anything, so even I stared at him to try and read where this was going.

"She's in one of her moods," I said. "Just go home."

"I'm not in anybody's mood," she said, starting to sweat. "Get away from him! I'm your mother. I take care of us."

"Mom, I'm just walking him to the door—"

"You are my child!" she bellowed, coming after me. James wasn't far enough behind me to be out of reach, so he stood between us. Mom swung at him and he held her wrist. "Miss Marguerite, I don't hit women. But I don't let women hit me."

Her eyes were wide. "Get out of my house! I'll call the police!"

He shook his head at her and let her wrists go. I looked at him, powerless.

"Call me," he whispered, and then he was gone, leaving me to fight with her. What she wouldn't do with her hands since I had stood up to her she did with her verbal abuse.

Slut. Whore. Bitch.

I picked up my keys in the middle of her tirade, tucked them into the back pocket of my shorts, and took off down the stairs into the street. It didn't matter that Dana was away at school and De La Salle was closed and there was no place for me to go. I could have walked the whole borough for the rest of the night. Mom interrupted the quiet of my brisk walk by wailing behind me like a siren: "Please come back! Oh, God. I love you, Shan! Don't leave me!"

I didn't turn back, not at first, even though I knew there wasn't any real escape. Thirty minutes later, I came back to the apartment, to Mom talking to two police officers standing in the hallway. She had reported me missing. "I can't control her! She does whatever she wants! I try as hard as I can but I swear, I don't know what to do."

"I'm sorry she called you," I said to the officers, walking past them into the apartment. "We're OK."

"Ma'am, was there violence here? Do you want us to file a report?" She had stomped back into the living room and flung herself on the couch. She was done. I shook my head. I thanked them for asking, and they left.

What they left behind was a pregnant fifteen-year-old on her way to an all-girl's boarding school with one more battle to fight. It felt like a life or death choice to me after all we had been through together. I could not imagine being a young mother, or having to take care of another person.

James wanted me to move to Florida with him so he could sell drugs and we could raise a family. Mom wanted me to stay with her in the Bronx, so she couldn't even pretend she was happy when I got the letter from Emma Willard saying I'd gotten a scholarship to attend in the fall. So when she read my journal one night when I was out with James, she was determined to use it against me.

We were high on the night air, humidity on our faces, when James walked me home. Marguerite, who never smoked in public, was perched on the dark steps leading to the front door of our building, puffing on a Newport. He saw the look on her face, her shoulders arched like a pissed off cat, and he turned around. "Bye," he muttered, and took off.

She ordered me in the house, where I saw the florid journal entry about my romps with James on the couch. Again, she didn't put her hands on me. What she did instead was far worse.

After hours of a long tirade, she woke me up early the next morning for a cross-town bus trip to James' house. I could hear his mother light a cigarette immediately after seeing Marguerite through the peephole in her door, and James refused to look at my mother as she read my journal entry aloud.

It was about sex in the shower. Sex in his mother's bed. Sex on the beach. Maybe I was pregnant. Maybe I wasn't. I just didn't care. All this was written in red felt tip pen in the pages of Mom's old Monroe College notebook that I was stupid enough to leave in a place where she could find it.

"They're kids," his mother said. "They have sex. Not always in my bed, but what are you gonna do?"

"I forbid her to see him again," Mom said, getting up.

His mother shrugged her shoulders and exhaled more smoke. James stayed seated, watching us with his eyes. I was so ashamed that I just looked him without saying goodbye.

Our last stop was Planned Parenthood, where Mom clutched that rosary of hers and said Hail Mary prayers loudly while I vomited up my Blimpie sandwich in the bathroom.

"Is it safe to tell her that you're pregnant?" the doctor asked me.

"Absolutely not."

They lied to her. I stopped writing in my journal, even after I had the abortion. I had been raised my whole life to be pro-life, and I wept for weeks afterward because I felt like a murderer. But I needed to get away from her. I needed my own future. I needed my own life. It was that baby or me.

For the first time in my life, I chose me.

CHAPTER 7
GET MONEY

Each eviction rolled into our lives like looming dark clouds of wildfire smoke. Each left us inhaling the charred remains of everything we left behind. For more than a decade, when Mom closed a door and turned the key, I turned to face the city with the nagging fear pulling at my stomach that we might never see the inside of that apartment again. It was a good thing we couldn't afford anything we would be attached to, except for the stacks and stacks of paper Marguerite hoarded.

Aside from a few worn cardboard boxes and trash bags of paper, we had only the essentials: a couple of towels; a few pairs of sheets; two kitchen table chairs to match a cheap, small table; and musty couches that sagged in their middles. Nothing belonged to us. Poverty made our lives and everything in them disposable. I believed for a long time that money would fix everything, and I learned from the world beyond my mother that work was the only way to get money.

That was how money became another saint to me and another main topic of my prayers. With money, I imagined a freedom that I craved more than regular meals. At twelve, when teachers started to ask me what I wanted to be when I grew up, I could not conceive of being anything but a writer, even though I suspected that came with its challenges.

I had no shame about my addiction to Jackie Collins and Danielle Steel novels—I wanted to write the bestselling fiction that they did, as improbable as that might be. I would settle for being a high school English teacher or maybe a professor, but what I really wanted was to find a way to get money so that I would never live with the kind of fear that defined my childhood. I would work as hard as I needed to for as long as I needed to doing whatever was in my power to do.

Writing was the first work I had that took longer but eventually paid off. Everything else was a gig. As a teenager, I won essay contests. The year I started college, I was published in a poetry anthology for the first time. I hoped these were signs of greatness.

My teachers encouraged me to keep writing. I loved writing and reading so much because they were portable ways to ease my loneliness and anxiety. The grown-up, logical voice in my head, the one that knew that Marguerite was not as good at earning money as spending it, refused to let me get carried away with my writing dream.

Mom said, "Everything you touch turns to gold, Shan. You can do anything you want to do."

By the time I reached my teens, I tried believing in the good things Mom hoped for. Whether I could turn words or stories into gold or not, I would do anything to ward off insecurity.

The danger of loss, even when we had nothing to lose, was constant, and I wanted away from that: the panic, the instability. I don't remember when I decided that part of breaking with the ongoing lack and trauma of my childhood would mean leaving Marguerite, but it started with understanding that the things she said and the way we lived were not at all connected.

Before I left the Bronx for Emma Willard, my first act of independence was going to work in the summer with the city's Youth Employment Program. Before I had a job, I would do nothing but wander, write, read, and sleep while Mom wandered the city without me, looking for God knew what. Like school, work gave my days a structure, a shape, instead of allowing me long hours of festering, searing dread. In the world of managers, supervisors, and other titles, I understood why Marguerite couldn't keep steady work—she did not take orders. I could take direction, but I secretly sneered at authority. Still, for a paycheck, I would endure the mind-rattling boredom of teamwork: working first as a journalist in a program at Hostos Community College, then as a summer camp counselor, and sometimes as a teacher.

I liked to listen, which turned out to be oddly rare, and I tried to talk as little as possible. As an intern, working in publishing and investment banking, I could easily work a sixty-hour week on little sleep or food. When I got tired or started to lose my patience, I remembered where I had grown up and with whom. It was not a distant possibility that I could remain stuck in poverty for the rest of my life.

Marguerite had probably never imagined our life together as it was when she was working regularly in Philadelphia, before I was born. In our family, her work ethic was legendary—it might have been the mania. But the mood swings that followed Jose's death made it almost impossible for her to keep a job. Mom was unapologetic about cursing someone out if he got on her nerves or showing up an hour later than work started. She was dismissive about employer complaints. "They're just jealous of my talent," she said. "Be careful, Shan. Sometimes people will just step on you because they're jealous of your talent."

When I started working, I could see that she had a point. In publishing, another black woman at the company where I worked introduced me to a group of professionals as the "Ho" at our company—an unfortunate shortening of my name in a public way that shamed and angered me so much that I left the room. At Goldman Sachs, where I worked in human resources for a summer, I was chided by my supervisor for wearing pants that showed off too much of my ass. There would be more and more incidents like this, usually under the watch of competitive women in the workplace, and they gave me an understanding of why some people chose not to work, especially in corporate circles.

But I was not like Mom, who was incapable of taking responsibility for behaving like two completely different women in the same day—a fact that must have alarmed her bosses. Consistency was my goal, even though I wasn't much for socializing or making nice. I did not stay after for drinks with my colleagues or ask about their children by name—I went to work, I went home, and I came back. I did not take sick days even when I was ill, and I did not believe in vacation.

Work could keep a woman sane and money could keep her fed. Marguerite taught me these things in spite of her failure to connect the two.

I knew early that I wanted writing to be my life's work, but the only black women I knew who wrote for a living were famous. They had names that were one or two syllables, beautiful to look at and easy to pronounce. As nice as it seemed to have money and fame, I was too practical even in my imagination to think about getting to a life like that from where I'd grown up.

I settled for what I knew was within my reach, jobs close to what I dreamed about but not the real thing. Shadow professions. I was afraid that the one thing I wanted the most in the world might be entirely possible, and then I'd have to let the world see me and my mother and our crazy past. Or maybe it was entirely impossible, and then I'd die destitute like Zora Neale Hurston, the brilliant black writer who attended Barnard and wrote, among other things, the beautiful classic *Their Eyes Were Watching God* but also died as a penniless maid.

When I got to Vassar on an academic scholarship, all that mattered to me was getting into Senior Composition, a selective group of several senior writers who would write a senior thesis of fiction or poetry. The campus, like Emma Willard, was a wonderland of students from wealthy families, beautiful vegetation and trees, and ornate buildings that had seen the likes of Jane Fonda and Jacqueline Kennedy. I worked in the serene and enchanting Thompson Memorial Library, replacing books in the stacks while inhaling the soothing scent of old tomes, and wrote in the dark cavernous dungeon-like rooms in the basement to get away from the swirl of activity above.

I took notes at every lecture, when Marcia Ann Gillespie or Elaine Brown or Afeni Shakur arrived, and eventually I started writing for the *Miscellany News*, our weekly paper. Until I started writing for the newspaper, my experience with journalism had been distant yet intimate, just like my relationship with my mother. I started learning to read by staring at the pages of the Philadelphia *Inquirer*, and at Vassar, I regularly devoured *The Nation* and the *New York Times*, since they were the literature available in our cafeterias.

Working at the *Miscellany* led to a column, and one of my columns was sent on a national wire. When an editor at the Enterprise Foundation read my reflections on navigating the world of Green Haven Prison, where I joined other students in talking to prisoners who were within months of being released about the world they were about to reenter, she asked me to write more for her online magazine, *Horizon*. My career as a journalist began with pieces published there, digital-only in 1998, and just like that I became a writer who was paid to write before I went on to become a full-time newspaper journalist the summer after I graduated from Vassar.

Journalism became my surrogate family when I earned the Hearst Fellowship. The hardest part was not leaving the East Coast, since I was becoming an expert at leaving. The hardest part about becoming a newspaper reporter was that it inserted the anxiety, the constant worry and panic that I carried as a kid caring for my mother, into my professional life. I was already tethered to my phone every time it rang, worried that Mom needed to hear my voice or she would call every hour until she finally reached me. After multiple evictions, I had become a seasoned nomad. If I failed at the job, I knew the worst that could happen would be the poverty and homelessness that I'd left behind in New York.

It was the perfect job for me, and the bonus was that I got to write for a living. I worked so much that I usually fell into bed in all my clothes. My paychecks were spent as soon as they arrived. Like Mom, I had no concept of saving for a future I wasn't certain I would live to see. I bought clothes I couldn't afford, I ran up thousands of dollars in credit card debt, and back in the days before unlimited phone minutes, Marguerite and I talked up a $1,000 bill.

It was the kind of thing I could have asked my father for, but he had stopped returning my calls or e-mails. When I met Victor, the power of money—for better or worse—took on even greater meaning. His life seemed to be the opposite of the one I'd experienced with Mom, and I hoped that knowing him would offer me a chance at the true nurture a parent should offer a child.

My father worked the same job for thirty years. He considered honest work to be the best spiritual practice a man could ask for. He didn't believe in God, he didn't celebrate holidays, and dreams to him were not miracles available for manifestation but abstract, frivolous ideas better left ignored. For him, work was the closest thing to prayer. He resented my writing, though. He didn't consider it real work. It was the main wedge between us.

I couldn't *not* write. The same way my father was nearly obsessed with his version of security, and my mother directed her attention at chasing her elaborate dreams, I devoted to getting money to support my writing habit.

Even after a lot of therapy, my relationships—with the exception of my friendships—were shallow. In my reporting work, I was exposed to gang violence, foster youth, parents in prison, and women in halfway houses, but nothing kept me up at night like the prospect of intimacy. I worried that getting close to someone made me vulnerable to the manipulation I was all too familiar with. Love felt like a trick to get me to take care of another person.

Money was straightforward and tangible. Relationships were unruly and undependable. At least at work, there was a logic to how things went.

Logic and love did not overlap in Marguerite's world.

"I might get married again," Mom would say in a singsongy voice. She was the queen of overstatement when it came to the man of the hour. The first of these was a Pakistani grocer named Raja, who visited us by walking a few blocks from the store he managed, not far from the train station. At first, he was just the friendly brown man at the store where Mom would let me get an Arizona Iced Tea in the tall can and an Almond Joy.

He was handsome enough, with his head full of curly black hair and his neatly trimmed mustache. Next thing I knew, Raja was visiting after sundown bearing a small paper bag filled with candy—Peanut M&Ms, Mary Janes, and lollipops. He brought Heineken for Mom. We once went to visit him in Queens, making the long trek from the two train to transfer to the west side, only to head out to a different borough altogether.

"What do you think, Shan, you think I look OK?" Marguerite emerged from his room wearing a sari. I don't know how she convinced this man that she was going to put on these beautiful layers of cloth everyday, but the orange material looked amazing against her skin.

"You look pretty, Ma," was all I said. It was actually the most beautiful I'd ever seen her. She never wore a sari again. It wasn't long before Raja was gone. He disappeared like our things, discarded by my mother like previous addresses. Before I could miss him too much, Mom was dating a flutist from an indigenous band that collected dollar bills and coins from commuters in an open guitar case above Grand Central subway platform in Manhattan. He looked like a Native American warrior, like the guy who played Chief in *One Flew Over the Cuckoo's Nest*. Mom had a crush on that guy too.

The musician had wide cheekbones that hovered over the straight line of his mouth like a beige, muscular cliff and straight hair that brushed his broad shoulders like a curtain. I think of him often in summer because he had come to visit us once after he'd performed a Sundance—a ritual that involved him suspending himself from a tree with hooks digging in the flesh of his back. He was so proud of the scars that he let Mom touch them with her fingertips while she smiled in awe. I grimaced.

One of the last of her paramours was a Russian portrait artist she met during one of her solo jaunts through Central Park. I never met him in person, so I was never sure that she didn't completely make him up, but he'd sketched her portrait more than once from the looks of the drawings she hid away in our closets. She wrote about the dreams she had about him on the walls inside the closet, too: "Vladimir and I may run away together."

Like apparitions, these men appeared for days or weeks then vanished. I knew nothing about them other than what Mom told me, which was often little more than their names. The prospect of love or romance, no matter how dead in the water it might be at first, changed her gait, just like when she'd gotten a check in the mail or won more than a few dollars in Atlantic City. Those feelings were probably like the highs she got from Dexatrim and Newports. They helped her slog through the other bullshit that came with everyday living, a poor woman's medication. If she couldn't have money or a house or a Bible bookstore, or any of the other things she dreamed about, she would have love. It wouldn't be long before she was in love again. Love for her was another world, a beginning that never ended, a meditation all its own.

CHAPTER 8

KNOW WHEN TO SURRENDER

S HUN RE: ADDITION TO MY E-MAIL I JUST SENT YOU ABOUT A HOUR AGO (SMILES, BUT SERIOUS).

SHUN I WAS ATTENDING SERVICES AND DECIDED TO TELL YOU THIS BECAUSE IT WAS LIKE A SPIRITUAL HEALING MESSAGE FROM YOUR GUARDIAN ANGEL (YOU KNOW EVERYBODY HAS ONE (SMILES, BUT SERIOUS) SO HERE GOES.

SINCE I AM VERY CLOSE TO MY FAITH I GUESS YOUR GUARDIAN ANGEL AND MY GUARDIAN ANGEL HAD A MEETING IN HEAVEN AND THIS IS THE RESULT OF THAT MEETING AND THEY WERE GIVEN INSTRUCTIONS BY OUR HEAVENLY FATHER FOR THEM TO TELL ME TO TELL YOU THIS MESSAGE.

WHEN YOU WERE A BABY AND IN 1979 I TOOK YOU AND THE REST OF MY CHILDREN DOWN SOUTH TO MEET MY FATHER AND WHILE HE WAS STILL ON EARTH HE LOVED MY CHILDREN SO MUCH AND ESPECIALLY YOU SHUNDA. I EVEN BATHED YOU IN THE BATHROOM SINK BECAUSE YOU WERE SO LITTLE.

ANYWAY SHUN THINKING BACK OVER THE YEARS WHEN I BROUGHT YOU INTO THIS WORLD BECAUSE I NEEDED SOMEONE SPECIAL IN MY LIFE AFTER LOSING ANOTHER SPECIAL PERSON, YOUR BROTHER JOSE. ANYWAY, THIS IS THE MESSAGE SENT BY OUR LORD. COMPARED TO THE AVERAGE 30 YEAR OLD YOU HAVE GRADUATED FROM ONE OF THE TOP COLLEGES IN THE NATION (VASSAR COLLEGE), YOU HAVE TRAVELED ABOUT 3 STATES AND DRIVEN TO THOSE STATES IN YOUR CAR. NOT EVEN THAT YOU HAVE MADE SURE THAT YOU KEPT IN TOUCH WITH ME YOUR MOM DURING YOUR VENTURE, BUT MOST OF ALL YOU HAVE KEPT YOUR JOURNALIST JOB, BUYING YOUR HOME AND NOW GOING BACK TO SCHOOL TO ACQUIRE BIGGER DREAMS AND FINANCIAL STABILITY FOR YOUR FUTURE. (BECAUSE I WAS UNABLE TO GIVE YOU SO VERY MUCH, BUT NOW LATER IN LIFE MY FINANCIAL SITUATION SEEMS TO BE GETTING BETTER).

IF THAT IS NOT GOD SENT SHUNDA I DON'T KNOW WHAT IS, YOUR EDUCATIONAL BACKGROUND FAR PASSES YOUR MOM'S, BUT I TELL YOU I AM PROUD OF YOU AND PROUD THAT OUR LORD HAS BLESSED YOU WITH SO MUCH FAITH, HOPE AND STRENGTH, NOW I BELIEVE THE MESSAGE IS THAT HE TOLD YOUR GUARDIAN ANGEL AND MINE IS THAT HE WANTS YOU TO CONTACT HIM, I KNOW THAT SOUNDS SILLY BECAUSE AS YOU SAY AND I BELIEVE YOU THAT YOU TALK TO GOD AND READ HIS BIBLE, BUT MAYBE, JUST MAYBE THERE'S SOMETHING MISSING, JUST TRY THIS PRAYER AND LET ME KNOW WHAT HAPPENS WHEN I E-MAIL YOU NEXT WEEK HERE GOES.

OUR FATHER, WHICH ARE IN HEAVEN, HOLLOW BE THINE NAME, THOU KINGDOM COME THINE WILL BE DONE ON EARTH AS IT IS IN HEAVEN. GIVE US THIS DAY

OUR DAILY BREAD AND FORGIVE US OUR TRESPASS AS WE FORGIVE THOSE WHO TRESPASS AGAINST US AND LEAD US NOT INTO TEMPTATION BUT DELIVER US FROM EVIL FOR THINE IS THE POWER AND GLORY FOREVER AND FOREVER AMEN.

REMEMBER YOU ARE VERY SPECIAL

(GOD BLESS YOU)

AND AS USUAL, I LOVE YOU WITH ETERNAL LOVE YOUR MOM

⇥⇤

Because Marguerite knew how to move and leap toward impossible things an ordinary mind would have ruled out, I learned that being a woman in the world meant tackling things most people considered impossible. When her mental illnesses were confirmed when I became an adult, it made the knot of anger and resentment that I had carried with me since I was a child start to loosen a bit. I was still usually annoyed with her when we spoke, because I just wanted her to be normal.

That was a selfish impulse, but I wanted her to be a normal lady so she might get to experience life without such sharp highs and lows, so that she could know peace. When she was kicking my ass and I prayed for her to die, I only wanted my life to be easier, and I didn't want to have to worry about her.

Medication seemed like one way. But even when she took medication, she didn't stay on it for long. And medication shut her off from her essence, the mania that made her so quirky and kept her undecided about making a final decision to worship me or want me gone. The broad love she painted on the canvas of us was always connected to Jose—I was his namesake, after all.

She couldn't have known the pressure that I felt to live up to the memory of a boy I had never met or how worthless I felt in comparison to his memory. Until I left her, I didn't give myself time to think about it either.

I fought with myself about leaving, even when I was gone. I had nightmares about boarding a bus only to get off because Marguerite was outside, screaming. That first time, I felt especially guilty. *What kind of daughter leaves her mother? Would God punish me with failure for leaving her alone to fend for herself?* Yes, she was a grown woman. But Marguerite had never really been a child. We had grown up together.

The knot in my chest as each departure approached was made from two tightropes: One was made of thick threads of hope that Mom would become a different, sane woman that it would be safe to adore. The other was made of hatred, shame, and rage. She would try three times to get me to untie that awkward knot—in high school, in college, and the year I turned thirty.

That knot throbbed and tightened for our whole trip to the bus station to Albany when I first left for Emma Willard with a lime green suitcase that Brother Brian had found somewhere. The luggage was light, since I didn't have much to bring: two pairs of jeans, a couple of button down shirts, old T-shirts, a dress I'd had since fourth grade, two pairs of socks, and a couple of books.

"I'll miss you something terrible," Mom said.

"It's not prison," I said. I would be back. I wasn't leaving forever, even if that's what I really wanted.

I was looking at the empty bus and she was looking at me like her heart was in her hands and I'd smacked it away so that it fell, so I added: "I won't be far."

"Four hours is far." She could be really lucid when she pouted.

"I have to go. I have to have my own life."

Mom looked at me blankly.

I kissed her soft cheek. I told her I loved her. I didn't look up once I was inside the bus.

The knot tightened.

Emma Willard was another planet from the Bronx, from New York City. Three meals a day in dining rooms with cloth napkins and sparkling silverware and girls whose families seemed richer than entire countries. The children of ambassadors and two-parent families, editors, professors, and me, keeping to myself, feeling more like an orphan than ever. *Please don't let them ask me what my mother does, please don't let them ask me where I live.*

James wrote once a week at first, then once a month, then not at all.

"You sound like a white girl," his mother said, blowing smoke over her shoulder, while James looked at me, trying to find the girl he had met a year ago in my face. He said I was becoming someone different, but I was only becoming more of who I really was. A girl who could hole up in the library for five hours binge reading and writing without stopping, gorging myself on safe silence. A girl who wrote bad imitation Langston Hughes poems and cheesy love songs and sketched drawings from old *Essence* magazines and counted the months from when I first got pregnant to mark every year my baby would have been born.

Mom tugged at the ropes in my chest with her disregard of school rules and curfews that made my poor house parents nuts. She called at all hours, the payphone on my dorm room hall ringing before sunrise and right after midnight, my classmates rubbing their eyes while knocking on my door and whispering, "It's for you. It's your Mom."

Phone calls and letters became her way of keeping us together even as I moved further into a different life, one that allowed me to forget her and New York City and our past for months at a time. My classmates were from Tokyo and Saudi Arabia and Rwanda. They spent weekends shopping at Crossgates Mall while I found a crew of eccentrics like me to visit thrift stores and art festivals and free author lectures. I faltered academically for a semester, certain I couldn't stay in this place where I obviously didn't belong.

Brother Brian sent money for snacks, and I worked in the bookstore and the development office, looking for a way to stay. I forced myself to stop thinking about the abortion, about my mother, about the Bronx. School became my life, the water I steeped myself in, a cliff to leap from to college.

Rita helped, even though she was still living in Egypt and had another baby on the way. We e-mailed each other monthly. It was a way to keep me connected to who I had been before. We were trying to write a new narrative of us. Marguerite and I tried too.

We think we know when something major is unfolding for us, and even in us, but one of life's cruelties is that you only know years later how moments will ease something for you, how they will force you to surrender the stories you'd rather cling to.

Marguerite surprised me by coming Parents Day weekend. Finally, she had chosen me over Atlantic City. It was the first time she had ever done something she'd said she would do. Carrying that bulging purse of hers strapped around her body, Mom tumbled out of a taxicab, her arms out as she smiled.

"I miss you! I love you! I'm here!"

She grabbed my face, looked into my eyes like she was looking in a mirror, and kissed me roughly on my cheek, leaving behind a lipstick mark that looked like a bruise. We walked around the campus grounds carefully, as if we had snuck into someone's mansion. I kept us away from the other families: fathers in blazers and mothers in floral dresses, their daughters pointing nonchalantly at the heavenly canopy of trees and the watchful eyes of Gargoyles.

In the dining hall, we sat in awkward silence. The last time we had eaten with a group of strangers, it was in a dark, sad Salvation Army dining room in Manhattan, but everything here felt so different: daylight streaming in, playful voices lilting in the rarefied air above us. We ate our food quickly, probably a force of habit.

I walked Mom through a few of the immaculate classrooms, the dance studio, and the library before we ended up sitting near the edge of campus under an old oak tree shedding blushed orange and maroon leaves which left a moist confetti carpet atop plush green grass. We sat on a marble bench that was gray and cool enough that I could feel it through my jeans. That knot had moved to my stomach now. When had it become painful to look at my mother and see how different she was—how different we were—from everything around us, no matter where we were?

Our bodies weren't touching. It felt like a whole world was wedged between us. Her shoulders were hunched and she uneasily placed her bag on the freshly cut grass. Without anything weighing her down or any good reason to get up or fidget, she put her hands between her thighs and smiled awkwardly at me, like she did when someone tried to take her photo. She looked young, her lipstick smudged a little at the corner of her mouth in a way that made me want to get a napkin and fix it.

She lifted the bangs from her wig away from her eyes with her thumb and her index finger. I asked her how she was feeling.

"Oh, Shan, you know me. God takes care of me. Are you still going to church?"

"No, I don't go."

"That hurts me," she said. "It really does. I see the other mothers in church with their families and I have no one."

"You have me," I told her. "I'm just not going."

After we sat there for a little while in silence, Mom grabbed her bag, as if she needed it for protection. She started rummaging through it for her lipstick. I asked, "How come you never talk about our family?"

"What do you want to know?"

"Tell me about Grandma. You always say that she had long hair."

"Hair so long she could sit on it," Mom said, showing off the gap in her front teeth. "She was the black sheep of the family. She died in a mental institution in Poughkeepsie. I was thirteen years old. She was really light-skinned and pretty, but being in South

Carolina, people didn't like that. Your grandfather, Makeba Wells, he was a professor. That's where you get your smarts from, you know."

"How did you deal with losing Grandma?"

"Oh, I don't know. What do you want me to say? It was hard. I became Catholic when I was eighteen. My Lord Jesus Christ protects me and keeps me."

We fell silent again. The other parents were leaving now. I wanted to hold her and not let her go, but I was also past wanting her to leave, so I wouldn't run into any of my other classmates while she was around.

"It's about dinner time, so we should go," I said, getting up.

"This is a beautiful campus, Shan. But I miss you something terrible." The sun was setting behind us in a vibrant orange as we walked across the lacrosse field. I knew a daughter should miss her mother, but I did not. *How do you miss someone who terrifies you?* We waited for a cab to take her to the bus station, though she insisted (until a security guard looked at her wide-eyed) that she might be able to walk to Albany from Troy: a fifteen-minute drive. She would call me when she got home, she said. I nodded. I let her give me another rough wet kiss, and I waited until the cab had disappeared beyond the gates to wipe her lipstick from my face.

The knot tightened again when Marguerite moved to Poughkeepsie my sophomore year at Vassar after she was evicted from our apartment on Daly Avenue. She put all our worn boxes full of paper and clothes in a storage unit in downtown Poughkeepsie and then moved herself into a room not far from campus. When she wasn't calling my dorm room at all hours, she would show up in the cafeteria so frequently that the servers who made me omelets or sandwiches knew her name.

Later, she worked as a cashier at the Stop N' Shop and showed my De La Salle Academy graduation picture to Vassar students and asked them to tell me hello. I would grit my teeth each time I heard from one of them and use the force of my oars in the water when I made the rowing team to try and let the anger that was welling up in me ease up. It didn't work. Neither did the full course load or all the student organization volunteering.

I would never see where Mom lived in Poughkeepsie; the Bronx had been the last place we lived together that was even close to home. I lived in my dorm room or on friends' couches during holiday breaks instead of going back to whatever dark place Marguerite claimed as home.

I was at one of the nation's most expensive schools, and my poor, mentally ill mother would show up bringing me a flimsy plastic bag full of toilet paper and fried chicken. The thought depressed me into drinking too much, leaving the crew team after a year, trying to escape my life by getting high every day. I kept writing—I couldn't help it, it was second nature—but just barely.

Just like I had in high school before I went to boarding school, I wanted to try and self-destruct, but something—God—was keeping me from going all the way. I kept working—at school, at internships, at writing. I figured if I stayed busy, nothing Marguerite could do or say would keep me from graduating. But what would happen after graduation? If I stayed on the East Coast, it was clear that she would follow me and I would never be free. But New York was all I knew; it was all I had ever cared about. The thought of going somewhere else had never even occurred to me until my life in newspapers came along to offer me an escape.

Marguerite was terrified of flying. Whatever that knot was in my body, I would lose it totally by leaving, I hoped. I could be another person. I could write a different story of us. Leaving, to me, had become second nature. It was a way of coping, a way of forgetting. It was the most surrender I could manage then.

Mom promised to call and write and maybe get on a plane for the first time in half a century—something we both knew would likely never happen. By then, I was deaf to her promises. I knew that they were made of bipolar and borderline narcissism, that they were more for her than for me. I asked her if we could talk once a week, an idea suggested by a therapist, and that became our routine. She moved back to Philadelphia—her Section 8 had finally come through—and she repeated to me her dreams: *I'm going to build a Bible bookstore and a community garden and when I get some monies, I'm finally going to move down South, back to South Carolina.*

You'll see.

The year I turned thirty, Marguerite called me from an Amtrak train in Philadelphia to tell me she was coming to Austin. I had moved there from the West Coast in 2005 to shift from newspaper journalism—the constant deadlines and phone calls making me feel like the whole world was just like Marguerite, every damn day—to a job as a librarian. I was also tired of reporting. It felt like I was fighting everyone every day: readers, editors, everybody.

While I had done the scariest thing for a formerly homeless person and bought a home, I considered marking three decades as a colossal failure. I was not married. I did not have kids. Work was my entire life.

I wanted to give myself back what I thought I had been missing, so I took myself to Disney World for a week. It was awful. If you are a single woman considering the same trip, don't do it. I came back to even more bullshit than I'd left: days that started at four thirty in the morning and didn't end until ten at night.

When Marguerite said she was coming for weeks, I did what I always did: I nodded; I said, "Sure, OK"; and I hung up.

Then, she called from a train in Chicago.

"We're going to Dallas. I know it's taking a long time, right? It is beautiful out here, Shan," she said. "I have to go, I only have a few minutes on my calling card. I will call you from Tex—" and the phone cut out.

She was coming to visit me in the one place I had rooted myself so that I would never see her again unless it was on my terms. I felt nauseated even as I cleaned the house. I couldn't sleep. My throat got itchy like a wool sweater was lodged in it. I couldn't breathe right. My eyes were red. I was likely just allergic to Austin—it happens when you've lived there long enough—but I felt like I was going to die. I tried Benadryl and Nyquil and everything else, but nothing kept me from the chills and sweats, and I couldn't sleep more than an hour at a time because of my cough.

I looked a mess when I picked Mom up from the train station. She stood outside in a thin coat with a worn plastic bag at her feet. "Don't look at my teeth," she said, a gloved hand rising to her mouth. A couple of teeth were missing in the front, and her bottom teeth rose like a tiny rickety fence. "I'm saving up to get them fixed."

"Is that all that you have to keep you warm?"

"Can we go to the store? I want some ice cream."

"Let's go tomorrow, Mom. I'm sick."

"What's wrong? You got a cold? You need to be wearing something around your neck."

We fussed at each other the whole time in the HEB grocery store on South Congress, where she added lima beans to her must-have, never-ending grocery list as I fumed and winced under the harsh fluorescent light. My coworkers frequented that store, and I wanted us to get in and out as quickly as possible, but Mom kept adding things she planned to eat for the week until I finally stopped the cart in the frozen entrées aisle and said, "You're killing me."

"Oh, Shan. Just one more thing, OK? Just one more thing."

Back at the house, she looked around my bare thousand-square-foot space and said, "I'm jealous. Your mom lives in a dump and you've got a lot of space down here. I wish I had that."

Maybe I shouldn't have been surprised, but I was alarmed that she would admit her jealousy. I coughed and said nothing before I crawled into bed and pulled the covers over my head. I wanted to disappear, and I wanted Marguerite to disappear, but it wasn't possible. We would have to be uncomfortable together. This was what I thought during a birthday brunch with some of my coworkers at Z-Tejas, when she looked at the menu and said, "I'll have whatever you'll have," and I snapped at her.

"Don't eat what I eat. Eat what you want."

"I want what you want, Shan." My coworkers smiled. I grimaced. I changed my order at the last minute, just to be spiteful.

Again, at the thrift store: "If I get something, will you buy it for me?"

"On my birthday? Absolutely not," I responded. Then she found a scarf she liked. I paid for it, muttering at her under my breath.

But the allergies had felled me, and I couldn't escape her watching the religious cable channels in the living room for hours at a time. I tried to sleep through it. I woke up at one point to her sitting at the edge of my bed with a steaming yellow mug. "Here, you should have this," she said. "It'll make your throat feel good." I looked down at the hot brown water with onion squares floating at the top and almost vomited.

"It's honey and hot water and onions," she added. "You'll see. It's good for your throat. Drink it while it's hot."

Drinking it made me want to die in my sleep. But the cough was gone, no doubt chased off by the disgusting onion-honey combo. When I got up to get water, I opened my cabinets to find that they had been rearranged.

Dishes and cups and glasses that had been put wherever they fit now sat in neat rows. The knot in my chest eased, the throbbing dull now. Mom was watching a documentary about Jesus.

"Why did you do this?"

"Oh, Shan, hush. This is the good part."

"But we already know how it ends."

"Shhhh!"

I made myself regular-ass tea with no anything in it but water and tea. I perched myself next to her and waited for the commercials. "Thank you for the cupboard. And for the…liquid thing."

"You feel better, right? I told you."

"Mom, you know why it's hard for me to have you here, right? You tried to kill me. You remember that?"

"I don't know. I don't remember. What do you want me to say? I was a bad mother, OK?"

How could something I remembered as being the reason for leaving her, my only justification for leaving her, be something that she didn't remember? I wanted to fight. She was being sweet and loving and my mother, and I wanted her to fight back. I wanted her to tell me she was wrong, I wanted to her to tell me I was right to leave and make my own life, no matter how lonely or afraid or depressed I was without her and away from her. Instead, she looked at those loosening tightropes and said, "I'm sorry I was a bad mother."

I sipped my tea and sat back on the couch and looked at her. I had learned that she was in her sixties by looking at public records at work, but she had never told me her real age. I mentioned that I didn't know stuff about her that women should know about their mothers. Like that. She said, "Well, I'm old, Shan. But I'm not *old* old. Why do we need to talk about this?"

I sighed. She had a point. I let the ropes start to untangle, painful as it was to surrender my righteous indignation. The questions I had were ones she couldn't or wouldn't answer. Not knowing it was the last time I would see her standing on her own, I drove us slowly to the train station, staring at the road ahead while she talked to me again about her dreams. When I left her there, she gave me one of those wet kisses of hers, and I hugged her as tight as that knot had been, and my chest felt light. Lighter than I'd ever remembered. I thought it was because she was finally leaving and my allergy attack was over and I would get to have my house and my solitude back. But it was more than that. I wanted to forget like she had forgotten. I was ready to surrender the past, even though I didn't know what or who we would be once I let go.

CHAPTER 9
LIVE ON YOUR OWN TERMS

2011

Marguerite loved to celebrate. You didn't have to take the party to her: she was the party. Lights flickered in her eyes, her mouth would curl up at the sides, and she'd nod her head and shake her shoulders to music, shuffling her wide feet with socks curled over her toes leaving her heels bare, side to side, off-beat.

In the house of her best friend in Philadelphia or in one of our many apartments, she liked the music turned all the way up, and she could easily get lost, her arms lifted up, fingers snapping. She loved Christmas the most. She would wash her favorite red blouse in the sink and hang it on the shower curtain to dry a day ahead of time.

She said an extra rosary for the season, dragging in real or fake trees some years just to have the lights around her. There were rarely gifts under the tree or even blankets to catch the shedding pine needles. She would say, "You're my gift. I'm your gift. Merry Christmas!"

When the door burst open the day we found her, light flooded into her Section 8 house, and it took a stretcher to lift her out of the dark. Rita had come for her.

Where she ended up at the end of her life was an affront to every celebration in her life. Torsos bent over laps in wheelchairs. Dull sunlight blocked by heavy curtains. It was no wonder Marguerite hated the nursing home.

There was no music there, no life. She would fidget, even as she got weaker. No, she wouldn't let the doctors X-ray her. Fine, she would get up on the table, but when it came time to hit the switch, she shifted and moved and wriggled.

To her, it didn't matter how far the cancer had spread. She knew death was coming every time she had to go back to the emergency room, every time she had to press the button to ask for more morphine. She was beyond ready for it to be over.

The doctors estimated that Mom had a few months to live. "Only God decides, Shan. Only God," she said to me on the phone. "I'm in so much pain. I know you just went through this with your father, but I'd rather be in heaven than here."

Heaven held Jose and Victor and all the land she wanted to plant tomatoes and okra. Heaven was a place of music and dancing and handsome men who looked like Charles Bronson. I had once prayed for her to be gone, but I was not ready to see her leave. "I'm ready to go home," she said.

"You're not going home, Ma," I said. "The doctors said you can't live on your own."

"Well, I need to talk to my lawyers." She was expecting a settlement from getting hit by a taxi in South Carolina. The company that owned the cab had since gone bankrupt. My sister and brother verified that this was actually a thing that was happening, not something she made up.

"I'm coming up there to see you soon," I said, changing the subject.

"It'll be good to see you, Shan," she said, and she chuckled, a high-pitched, muffled sound, maybe because of the tubes. "Don't be scared. I lost a lot of weight."

Suddenly, I was a little girl again, and the only person in the world who could protect me was my Mom. In real life, she had not always been good at that. But all these years later, on her way to death, she was still trying. "I just don't want you to suffer. I love you," she said.

I told her I loved her. I had to go. I was getting ready for work. "Hang up," she said. "You know I don't like to hang up first."

We usually scrambled for food and warmth during Christmastime in New York City. The scalding radiators in our apartment were loud, rusty pieces of shit that sent steam spraying toward the ceiling in loud squeals. The refrigerator was often empty, but Brother Brian or church volunteers usually made sure we didn't go hungry on Christmas. We made turkey and stuffing and plopped in front of us on a couch or plastic chairs to set in front of a TV where we watched *It's a Wonderful Life* or the *Charlie Brown Christmas Special* or *Rudolph the Red-nosed Reindeer.*

"You kind of look like him, Shan," Mom said.

"The reindeer?"

"Your nose gets red like that in the cold," she said. She started to crack up, and the gap in her front teeth showed.

"No, it doesn't," I said, smiling shyly at her.

"It does, and you have a dimple on your forehead too."

"You know a lot about my face!"

"When you frown I can see it. It's cute, Shan," she would say. "It's where your brother kissed you before you were born and came to me from heaven."

Most years, instead of decorating with lights at home, we went to see the city's most famous tree at Rockefeller Center, a few blocks from Saint Patrick's Cathedral. It towered over the ice skating rink below, and both Mom and I stared wide-eyed at it, year after year: the giant, multicolored bulbs, the dark space between the branches, the giant toys. It was the real-life version of what she imagined a good monument to Christmas to be, better than any replica she could try to make with her hands.

"All we're going to do is look at it?"

She said breathlessly, nodding, "It's beautiful."

Years before our last Christmas, I tried for the last time to have a holiday with my mother like the ones my friends told me about. Inside her Section 8 house, she had taped a picture of Jesus she had ripped from a calendar to the wall in front of the door. It had lipstick smudges where she had kissed it, and her lovely script declaring him her Lord and Savior: a love note to God.

Beside it, next to a sagging couch, was a karaoke machine Manny had stored with some of his other things when he moved from Atlantic City to the New Jersey suburbs. On a side table, a cheap plastic phone doubled as a paperweight for an envelope with the names and phone numbers of her children scribbled on it.

Rita, her husband Alphonso, and I sat down with food they'd brought from home to share with her in her dimly lit kitchen. She was wearing what she always wore—a skirt that barely covered her knees and clung to her wide hips, a blouse that amplified her belly bulge. Her nails were caked over with old remnants of nail polish almost as thick as her yellowing nails.

Rita and Alphonso and I were all stiff, our faces sullen. Mom was upbeat and grateful for the food. She was slowing down, even then. After, Manny would help her move the mattress down to the kitchen, so she wouldn't have to climb the stairs to go to bed.

Our last Christmas together, I woke up in the house of a family friend in Philadelphia, getting ready for church after a house full of children had been up for hours ripping open presents and running around the house. I had been sleeping on a twin bed in Rita's home for almost three weeks, missing my own bed back home in Austin but afraid to leave since we didn't know how long Mom would be alive.

My phone broke around the same time, and Rita teased me about the way I wrestled with the broken buttons before giving up. I held onto it for a few days too long because everything in the world seemed broken. Mothers leave their children; they die before we do, yes, but Marguerite was not yet old enough yet to leave me. Our lives were still broken in a way I believed only she had the power to mend.

I sat next to Rita at Stronghold Baptist Church, and I wept. I could only really cry in two places by then, in the house of God and at my mother's bedside. For all my traveling and adventures, for all my ambition and making my way in the world, I was still a frightened little kid. We were in a season of celebration, and it felt like a betrayal to smile or give gifts. It felt like a betrayal of my mother's life to even breathe, to just keep living my life as if it had meaning without her in it.

I needed the word, the exaltation of something much bigger than me, than us. I needed the infusion of glory and spirit, some light in a season of darkness to baptize me in a hopeful future. The present was breaking my heart. Whatever was coming for Marguerite had to be better than what she was feeling now. I was sitting in the pew with my sister, but my heart and mind were with Mom in that nursing home, so I asked Rita to take me there.

I cried tears of anger, release, and surrender. What if Mom made it through, by some miracle that she had always talked about, and she took medication, and we could be, finally, like all mothers and daughters? She hadn't guided me like mothers are supposed to, but dear God, I was here and breathing and by most accounts a good human: that was something.

Hours later, I sat at my mother's bedside. She had shit on her wrist again, which Rita wiped off with hard tissue. Mom's wig was in the corner of her cubby. Rita sat staring at the television while I held Mom's hand. Her fingernails were yellow but soft now; her fingers as thin as mine.

"I'm so happy to see you," she said. She talked again about coming into money, about wanting to move into her house. "Maybe not that house. Well. God will take care of us," she said, finally. She was high on morphine, and her eyelids would drop mid-sentence, like she was about to go to sleep.

I moved my chair up, trying to get close to her face. She couldn't understand what I was saying when I asked what happened to her scarf. She was wearing a towel over her cropped gray hair.

"So are you going back to work or what?"

"I'm going to write." I didn't want to waste anytime talking to her about my future, knowing that she wouldn't be around to see it.

"That sounds nice," she said. "When are you coming back?"

After you're gone, I thought. *The next time I'll be here is during your funeral.* My eyes welled up, and I remembered that she hated to see me cry.

"I don't know," I said. I realized then that I could tell her what I wanted to tell her without saying goodbye. "I'm going to miss you very much," I said. I told her I was leaving Philadelphia in a few days. In my head and in my heart I added, *Goodbye.*

She touched my arm. I rubbed hers, which was too thin, and moved from the chair to sit on the side of the bed, while she mostly stared at the television. She was curious about the coffee cup I had brought in with me. She looked at it and then me, and then she smiled, and I felt like she really saw me and really understood where my heart was. I smiled back at her, the most light I could muster.

"I love you very much," she said.

"I love you, too, Mom," I answered. I closed my eyes. I thought, *I forgive you. God, please don't let her feel too much pain.*

I hope this is enough, this sitting with her and kissing her on the forehead and letting her kiss me on the cheek. She started to nod off. We left the nursing home, and for the rest of the night, I was in a fog. I wanted Christmas to come and go because I knew Marguerite wouldn't live to see another one. It took several hours for me to fall asleep.

⇒‡⇐

CHAPTER 10

TAKE GOOD CARE

2012

Rita and I talked by phone daily into the New Year, when I was back in Texas. Our conversations got shorter and more intense. Mom was running a fever; then she stopped eating. After a few days of silence, we talked about what to do with Mom's body—cremation—since she hadn't said what she wanted after she died. We had to think about the end, coming any day now, and I tried not to stay in bed. I put my hands in the dirt of my garden, trying to stay connected to the world of the living.

Six days before I turned thirty-four, a couple of friends I never get to see came to my neighborhood to enjoy a beautiful seventy-five-degree January day with a hike through McKinney Falls, a state park oasis ten minutes from my house teeming with waterfalls and beautiful trails. They brought their little boy and a big dog and I brought my dog, Cleo. I bought a ticket to go see *The Descendants* without knowing anything about the movie. We had been walking for a little longer than five minutes when my cell phone rang. It was my sister.

"I'm just calling to let you know that Mom passed away this afternoon," she said, her voice thick with tears. It was around one o'clock in the afternoon. She said Mom's friends and family had gathered around the same bed where I'd kissed my mother good-bye, singing and praying when Mom lifted her arms and took her last breath.

I don't remember what I said; I only know that I stopped walking. My eyes were watching Cleo explore some rocks and sniff around the park below a barren waterfall. The rock beneath what was usually a heavy stream was so prominent because of the long drought of our intense summer. It looked like a desert landscape.

I couldn't process it all right then, so our conversation was brief. I was stunned and oddly determined to still go to the movies. I wanted my life to keep going like nothing had changed even though I knew everything had changed. Rita told me she would call back and we could talk more about the memorial service and how we would work it all out later.

My friends hugged me, one at a time. Anything I needed, they insisted, I should let them know. We kept walking, admiring the wild cacti and the bald trees and the clearings between forest and narrow trails. After about fifteen more minutes of this, of saying maybe I wasn't crying because I knew that eventually Mom would be gone, I asked them to take me home.

I took Cleo home and then drove to the movie in silence. I was not crying. I was not listening to music. *The Descendants*, starring George Clooney, one of my favorite actor crushes, is centered around the story of a terminally ill mother. Someone who had seen it warned me that it might hit too many of my personal buttons. "I wish someone had warned me," she said, because she had lost her mother too, and it was an unexpected shock to see the graphic nature of a mother's death on screen that way.

I'd bought the ticket because I knew I needed to cry. At some point, I would force the tears that were living in my body, in a knot, like a gang of sadness behind my heart, to come on out. The movie helped me get there, and my sniffles joined the chorus of tears in the dark that rose and fell with the sad scenes of another distant life.

On my way back home, I called my sister. I wanted Mom cremated. I wanted her ashes here with me, wherever here was going to be. I had been a nomad for a month or more, I had been the nomad she made me all my life. She could keep wandering with me, I reasoned. It was my last chance to fight for her as I remembered her.

But before I could say anything, Rita said this: "She'll be cremated this afternoon, and then I was thinking we could spread her ashes on a lake not far from where I live."

I felt like hugging her. This was how big sisters saved the lives of their little sisters…moments at a time. I had wondered what all the fuss was about, but in that moment, it became clear to me that she had done this for me again and again throughout my life, that she had been rallying to protect my little stone-pocked heart from whatever threatened it for over thirty years—whether I knew the details or not.

"That sounds good. That's what I was thinking," I said, smiling.

"And you have the farthest to come, and the funeral home people said that we can have the memorial service whenever we want, so we'll have it in a few weeks to give you time to get a ticket and come back," she said, her voice strong. She was such a caretaker, my sister. I felt like I didn't really deserve her.

So that was that. I went off to buy food. A baja shrimp taco and chips and green chile queso from Torchy's, a place I had once visited too much. I bought cupcakes from Sugar Mamas bakery— piña colada and red velvet. I called people to tell them that mom was gone. I went to the store to get Frosted Flakes and milk and walked out with the shrimp-flavored ramen noodles mom used to make and a jar of pickles.

I watched *Weeds*. I talked on the phone. I realized that I was uncomfortable in my body.

I didn't want to rest. I had a couple of glasses of wine. I mentioned her death to some close friends on Facebook, and the texts started. Then I told more people the next day, and the phone calls began again.

I didn't necessarily want to share my grief, and I didn't know what I needed. To be in my house, still, reflecting on her life. Thinking about us. I sent pictures of her that I had acquired, but there were just three of them—she had always had a superstition about photos. I took one photo of her in our Daly Avenue apartment. She was in a striped white and navy dress with big brass-looking buttons down the front, smiling a forced smile that made her eyes big and wide. Her thick, short nails were caked over with old maroon nail polish, her lips red with lipstick that had mostly worn off.

There was a similar picture of her with my niece Rachel, taken in 1996. Rachel was tiny then, a hugger like my nephew Joshua. Mom was looking off into the distance and Rachel was looking at her with a sly grin, like Nana was being silly—which was probably true. The last picture, the one that left a black rectangle of emptiness where the other photos had been, was a regal one. Her hair was pulled back in a stunning fluffy ponytail at the nape of her neck. She was thin and stoic. I can't begin to describe the dress—it was one of those sixties/seventies numbers, like a quilt mini dress with a belt. Her legs were long and shapely. It was the way I wanted to remember her. Fierce and beautiful.

In church, at home, running on the trail around Lady Bird Lake in the days that followed, I continued to wrestle with the fact that I had been writing about us—and really both of my parents—for my whole life. Now, there was just me. I was the keeper of our adventures and stories. I was free to tell the whole thing, exactly as it was. All I wanted to write about, though, was Mom's goodness to me, how much of a fighter she was in spite of a life that never quite aligned the way lives are supposed to. The smothering love that I never felt worthy of, enmeshed as it was with the love of my brother Jose, who was also gone. She was with him and my father in heaven, I hoped, reunited with them as she had longed to be for so much of her life.

The weight of that responsibility scared me. The sadness of going back through my unreliable and sentimental memory worried me. The words were gone, I said, and sometimes that was true. Most of the time, I was not prepared for the tenderness of my own words or feelings. I did not trust them not to betray me, not to flood over with the mythology of my mother, especially since both the people who created me were now dead.

I wanted them to all be beautiful and to come out exactly right, but I was a mess and I knew that was too much pressure. I was special, my mother would always remind me. Never forget that.

I was too aware of how special she thought I was, and under the weight of my sadness, I didn't care very much about it at all. I wanted to be ordinary, mediocre. I wanted to live a life that honored her, but I could think of a million ways to do that and none of them would bring me back the phone calls that annoyed me at the time or that out-of-control laughter or the sweetness of the few minutes a year when I felt like she really heard what I was saying to her and understood.

﹦﹢﹢﹦

I would spend the next year and a half trying to identify who I was as an official orphan instead of an unofficial one. Without knowing it, my immediate reaction to grief and sorrow was extreme self-care. I would spend the next year living off of my savings and freelancing full time, barely leaving the house except to walk the dog and to travel a little for writing conferences.

The very first thing I did was put dozens of plants in the ground. This was immediately soothing. With a friend who recently lost her

brother to a heroin overdose, I wandered the oasis of a local nurs-
ery in the middle of a weekday, marveling at roosters and hens,
donkeys and goats. I bought trailing lantana, a bunch of Texas
sweet onions, two kinds of mint, and a few floral-looking bunches
of lettuce.

My thirty-fourth birthday began with me staring at the garden.
I had started that garden reluctantly, with no idea what do other
than what my gut told me about rich soil and watering plants deeply. For someone who loves life instructions in the form of self-help
literature, I am strangely resistant to reading instructions about
plants. I feel like the spiritual component of planting is believing
that the plants will tell you what they need and you can give it, even
in extreme heat and drought, or you will pay the price with their
little charred branches and wilting leaves.

The morning of my birthday, I spoke to Brother Brian. He
remembered the look on my face one Thanksgiving when Mom
didn't have any food in the house, but she was telling him an elaborate story about what she hoped would happen. "You just gave me
this look like, 'She's crazy but she's my mother,'" he said with a ro-
bust chuckle. "She loved you more than anything, God bless her."

We talked for a few minutes before the birthday celebrations
began in earnest. I was heartbroken, but the cracks in my usually
strong facade were filled with the love of my former coworkers and
colleagues who bought me food and journals and drinks. A decadent lunch with a friend was followed by an hour-long nap and a
gathering of about twenty of my friends, mainly from the newspaper, who stopped by to buy me beer and Jack and Coke.

It was weird to celebrate in the midst of grief. It was almost as if
the world was supposed to pause while I concentrated all my energy on mourning. As if human beings can always only feel one emotion at a time. As if there was some kind of shame in celebrating
the fact that I no longer had to live in the shadow of my mother's
own lifelong struggle with grief over Jose, grief over a life she was

never going to have, even if she fabricated the life she wanted every day with her words.

I listened to Stevie Wonder over and over again all morning—"All I Do," a song that is filled with joyous horns and Stevie's silky, giant voice. I danced. My sister sent along some pictures of me with mom, taken sometime in the 1990s at her friend Frieda's house—the same one who had done her nails and bought her a wig when she was at the nursing home.

When I wasn't dancing and drinking, I would just look at them, remembering how much she had loved to dance. She mainly lifted her shoulders in time to whatever beat there was and showed all of her teeth when they were even and mostly white.

None of the craziness I had lived through or things that I had survived with and without my sister around troubled me. When my birthday was over and I had worn myself out partying, what un-nerved me and kept me up at night was that I could now have the life I wanted, the one I said I had been waiting to start as soon as I was far away from my mother's chaos.

I applied for international and national fellowships that would suddenly make it possible for me to realize my long-time dream of living in two places, or at least, having more than one home. For someone who had never had a home for longer than a few months or years at a time as a kid, and then throughout my twenties, this idea seemed disastrous and maybe even overly optimistic. What about the logistics? What about my dog? What about my bills?

"You can never be homeless again," a friend said to me over margaritas. "You know how to take care of yourself. There is a big difference between then and now."

I had not cried in a couple of days. So the tears snuck up on me after a little tequila in a pretty container, with this friend with beautiful hazel eyes, piercing and so kind. I wept, I finally got more than two hours of sleep, and I vowed to allow myself to start letting go, really, of me and my mother. Just a little at a time. As much as I might need. Who knew how much it would turn out to be?

━┽ ┾━

The Saturday morning of the memorial service, about three inches of snow had fallen by the time my sister's southern New Jersey house started creaking under the footsteps of my family waking up. I had been in bad spirits the day before, angry.

All my defenses—alcohol, mostly—were in Texas, and I was on the East Coast, where it was twenty-eight degrees and people were being annoying. Beautiful bouquets of flowers, some dead, others half alive, were in the living room, the kitchen, and the dining room of my sister's house. A stack of more than thirty cards had arrived from her church family, and they offered our family a thick envelope of an offering.

We did not yet have Mom's ashes. We were busy paying for the down payment for the hall near Johnnie Ann's house on Fifty-second Street. I was angry that someone wanted to hire a nurse in case people fell out during the memorial service. I was irritated that now my mother's life had come to pass and all of a sudden, I had to share her with people who had only known her from a distance.

In death, people hold one another close. It is a selfish, irritating act. We remember, looking at another's mortality, that we don't have all the time in the world to love each other enough. Maybe one day we will have that luxury, in the land of the living, we think. But in the world between here and the hereafter, there is a space that intention cannot bridge.

I had distanced myself too, which made this irritation of mine, this self-righteousness, all the more irritating. I was irritated with people who grieved her, while at the same time I was aware that I could not and should not try to control their process. And I was irritated with myself for being irritated. Meditation was helpful. The morning of the memorial service, I woke up without an alarm at 6:20 and breathed through a series of Metta phrases: *May I be free from enmity and danger, may I have physical happiness, may I have mental happiness, may I have ease of well-being.* I wished for that for friends, for relatives, for my mother.

The tears fell again—short streaks that dried on their own, like Amy Winehouse sang. I am usually the last one dressed, but this morning I was the first to get up, get in the shower, pull my make-up and hair thing together, and get downstairs to sit on the couch and wait for the day to unfold.

Rita dressed in a turquoise blouse and a long turquoise skirt. She looked at my black outfit and just said, "Black, huh?" She was not going to cry or mourn, I figured. But this would be our funeral for Mom anyway.

Rita's friends and family from Christian Stronghold, her church for over thirty years, were fully in our service at the Bible Way church. Someone had made us quiche and sticky buns for breakfast before the service. Someone mercifully brought Dunkin' Donuts coffee. I sat and stared at one of the programs with a picture of my mother in a cute miniskirt set. It had been taken so long before I knew her. I had stolen that picture from my father before I left him for Texas.

High school and college buddies popped up, and tears sprang into my eyes without my control. I was so moved to see them. My uncle Larry, my favorite cousin, Maria. A dozen uncles and aunts and friends of my mother I hadn't seen in decades.

The service was uplifting, a tribute to Mom's journey to go be with God. Mostly, I cried during the gospel songs, which is my way. I tried to imagine her hanging out with my brother and my dad, her talking face to face with her Creator, finally, after seventy-two long years of one tiring emotional, financial, or spiritual battle after another. My eyes were weeping, but my mouth smiled.

It helped that my sister and I share a unique sense of humor. When someone went over the allotted two minutes to talk about how much my mother loved parties and celebrations, Rita managed to kick me on the sly, even though we were sitting in the front row. My auntie Janie, in a white sequined blouse, took the microphone and stepped away from the lectern and proceeded to talk about the good fruit Margaret had borne.

"Their brother Leonard couldn't be here because he's in rehab for multiple sclerosis," she said.

I almost snorted. My brother Leonard had been in a home since the age of eight. He had cerebral palsy.

I had to stop looking at Rita because she was in full on fed-up big sister mode, being gracious and composed while sometimes also looking out of the corner of her eye at me as if to say, "What is this mess?"

My mother's best friend was the one to whom I felt the most drawn. I learned why not long after I walked over to her. I said to her that I just wanted to thank her for taking such good care of my mother. I knew that the wig and her nails must have made her feel young and womanly again, like the end wasn't too far off, but she still wasn't "*old* old," as she liked to remind me.

"That was my girl," Miss Frieda said, smiling and crying too.

Later, before she left, she came over to me and asked if there was a place where we were keeping things that had belonged to my mother. I told her I didn't know, and she put in my hand a beautiful white rosary I knew must have meant the world to my mother. I almost cried again. It was like she had handed me a bridge back to my mother. I hugged her and kept the rosary with me over the next few days, carrying it around with me in my purse along with my meditation beads.

She wasn't gone. She always said, after all, that she would never leave me.

CHAPTER 11
HONOR YOUR OWN RESILIENCE

My heart is the underdog I am always rooting for.

I remembered this as I sat at my kitchen table in Austin three years ago. I had tried to run longer than two miles after finishing three marathons in a year as an amateur runner and knew that my flesh was up to the task but my mind was not. Tears sprang up while I wrote about how liberating it was to decide that I could stay broken or I could go somewhere and try to put my life back together.

The most immediate, lasting influence of the death of my parents was that I came to view change with less resistance. Once, when I was younger, I wrote out five-, ten-, and fifteen-year plans with a mixture of certainty and willful hope. I kept aggressive track of time—two paper calendars and planners in addition to two digital ones.

Grief makes time slow and still. It puts moments in perspective.

I never abandoned God like I had abandoned church, but I did learn to watch for God in what I might normally consider co-incidence. Butterflies, blue jays, a rainbow after a severe storm. It was nice to remember the abundantly beautiful things in creation. Their existence reminded me that there was still so much left to love and care about in the world.

I realized that when my parents were alive, I spent so much time trying to prove my worthiness to my father and to prove the importance of life to my mother that I gave myself over to the thoughts and feelings of others. Before, it seemed like other people's opinions of me were so much more important that my own opinions and thoughts. Now, I liberated myself from the prison of other people's perceptions—at least, I tried harder to remember that what people think of me is not only not my business but it is not something that is consequential to the quality of my life.

Speaking of liberation, there is something extraordinary about the death of your parents that is simultaneously devastating and freeing. The one remaining person I wanted to love and accept me no matter what was my sister Rita, and she had already told me that there was nothing I could do that would keep her from loving me.

That was all the permission I needed to rebuild my life.

After my mother's death, while I burrowed into my home in Austin with my dog, Cleo, I began blogging about the single life. That blog became my first book. Writing was the life raft for me that it had always been, except this time I was counting on it to help me keep me and the dog fed and to supplement my savings so that I wouldn't have to go back to an office before I could really handle it.

It was a gift to be able to spend the year focused on doing exactly what I wanted to do. I didn't feel a single ounce of guilt. I made room for my grief and for my gift—I went to my first and only Voices of Our Nation Arts workshop, a writing workshop for people of color. I spent half of my time there incredibly grateful that I had finally been admitted to one universally known and honored space for other writers of color, which includes the likes of cofounder Junot Diaz, my friends Vanessa Martir, Aya De Leon, and Suheir Hammad among many, many others. The other half of the time, I felt like I was poking around in the fresh wound that was my mother's sudden absence from my life, even if it hadn't been sudden at all. I was writing about her, about us, the way she moved in the world, the fact that she was now forever gone.

By the end of the week, I left unceremoniously, eager to get back to my safe place.

The rest of 2012 was, frankly, a blur of writing and editing, hiding from the world and peeking out every now and then to see if I still resented the fact that it was going on as if Marguerite were not the center of everyone's life. I resented it less and less as time went on, but a key feature of my grief, and one that I respected, actually, was that that resentment—that chip on my shoulder—became a main feature of my existence. I did not try to push it away.

In 2013, I started to leave the cocoon I had made for myself. I threw a party for singles when I published that first book. I took a job at the University of Texas doing communications work. I thought maybe life was starting to look up.

A strange thing was happening. In work and in love, I was attracting people I had to walk on eggshells around. It was true of my supervisor, a middle-aged white woman who told me during my first weeks on the job that she was worried that people would like me better and replace her with me. It was also true of a long-time flame from over a decade ago with whom I reunited and who offered me delicious, sultry affection without commitment. He was always present via text, but in real life, he was not truly available— the story of my life that I wanted desperately to rewrite.

I joined a sports league and bowled. I tried volleyball again. I'm horrible at both, but it didn't matter. I was trying to find my footing in the world, even while I was nursing my heartbreak.

It only took a few months before the job took a bad turn. My position was eliminated in a reorganization in September. In October, inexplicably, the roof started to leak, promising to be an expense that I did not need. In November, Cleo died.

"OK, God," I said aloud. "I get it. I'm leaving."

I had dreamed for many years of returning to New York City, but my mother's life and her mental illnesses meant that she was likely to show up wherever I was. I had spent my whole adult life running and moving away from her insanity, even though, as sad as it made me after her death, that meant putting so much physical distance between us and between me and everything that I knew and loved that brought me comfort and joy.

It was the partial culmination of a dream for me to leave Texas and move to Washington DC. In the nation's capital, I reunited with my family of friends who were both living in the area and beyond. I was back in an East Coast city, a place where people knew what it was to fight long, hard battles and remain yourself—at least some of them.

My friend Elizebeth drove with me from Texas. We arrived in the city on the day that Beyonce's first secret album dropped, which to me was a good omen. That Christmas Eve, I attended mass at the Basilica and wept for me and my mother. There were so many people that it was standing room only in the main part of the Basilica, but I found a place to sit in one of the alcoves dedicated to a saint. This one was green with a familiar face: St. Patrick. When I looked up and strained to listen, I smiled and thought, *This is exactly where I am supposed to be.*

In DC, I found the parts of myself I had forgotten. I sort of stalked my family, ecstatic that I could get to them now by car instead of plane. New York City is home, so it's family, too, and whenever I walk the streets I wandered with and without my mother, it helps me patch up my grief—or maybe just befriend it while I walk through Central Park and the Metropolitan Museum and rock with it on the subway.

DC is not perfect. The winters can be brutal. The Metro is an easy target to complain about. This is a town where ambition is worn on the sleeve and tribalism peppers the language.

At the same time, it is a majestic place. History is evident in the architecture, the diversity is global, and proximity to power is tangible. All these things remind me that history does not have to only be a story of failure and heartbreak. It also contains beauty, passion, and all the things that make our lives worth infusing with more of the same.

When people tell the story of running, particularly long distances, they tell it as though it is only about struggle, fatigue, and resilience. But there are moments of radiance too. I felt that in my first DC race the spring after I arrived here, when the cherry blossoms began to open and the frozen breeze reminded me that I was closer to recovering my self than I had ever been. Almost every stride reminded me that I had left behind a litany of disasters, that I had never even really needed a reason to do what I needed to do for my own repair. The road back to myself began with deciding that I would not be defined by my broken places. I had been on this journey for over twenty years without realizing that it was as simple as heeding the call of my heart and my gut to do what it takes to be defined by something more, something else.

ABOUT THE AUTHOR

 Joshunda Sanders is a writer whose previous works include *All City*, *How Racism and Sexism Killed Traditional Media: Why the Future of Journalism Depends on Women and People of Color*, and *Single & Happy: The Party of Ones*. *The Beautiful Darkness* inspired her TED talk about the dual stigmas of poverty and mental illness around the globe. She lives in Washington, DC.